SPIRITU/
ACC
ST. PAUL OF THE CROSS

MW01614647

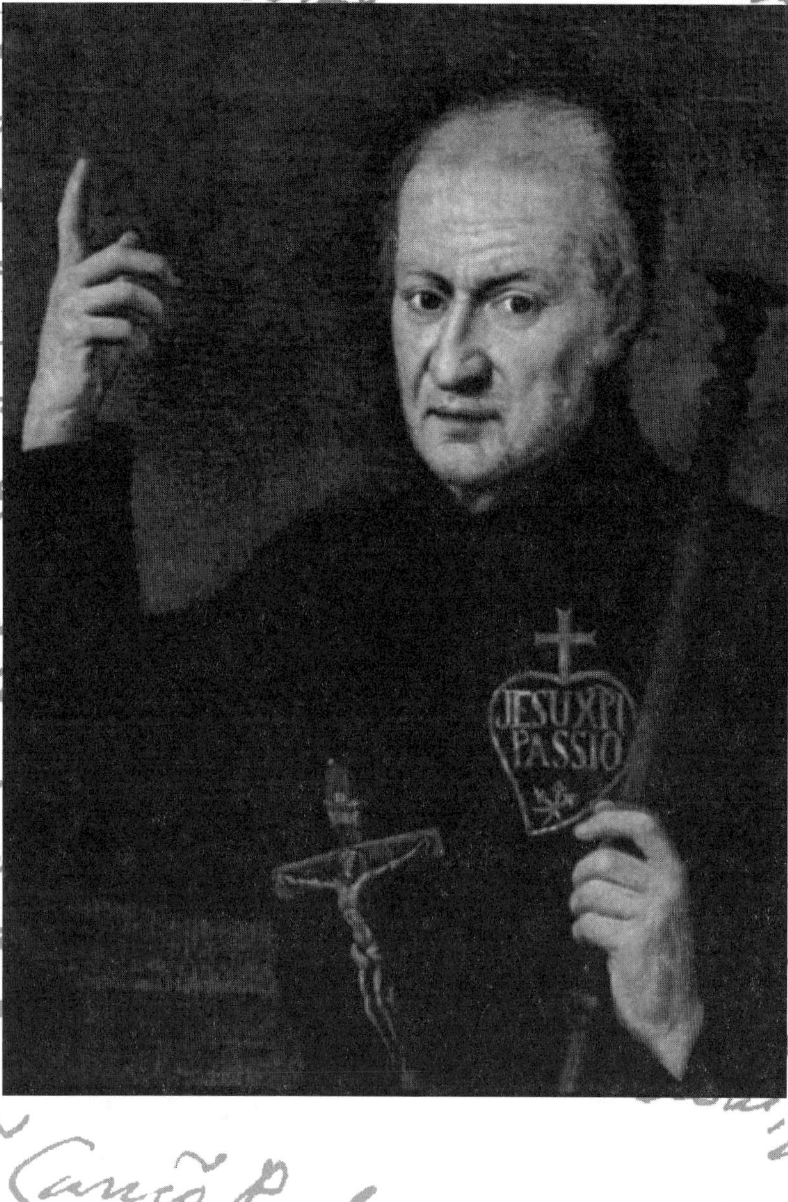
JESU XPI
PASSIO

Spiritual Direction
According to
St. Paul of the Cross

A practical commonsense approach...

Bennet Kelley, CP

Passionist Press
Union City, New Jersey
USA

Cathy Metts

References in this book are nearly all to the letters of St. Paul of the Cross from the Italian edition: Lettere di San Paolo della Croce. Rome. 1924,1977. The Roman numeral indicates the volume and the Arabic number the page.

An English edition now exists: Letters of St. Paul of the Cross, 3 volumes, Translated by Roger Mercurio, C.P. & Frederick Sucher, C.P. Edited: Laurence Finn, C.P. & Donald Webber, C.P., New City Press 2000, available at www.crossplace.com

PASSIONIST PRESS
526 Monastery Place
Union City, NJ 07087
Tel: 888-806-6606   www.crossplace.com

© Passionist Press, Inc. 2008
All rights reserved
Database right Passionist Press (maker)
Originally published by Alba House, NY, 1993

ISBN 978-0-9815918-1-0

I would like to express my great gratitude
to Jean Wilson & Susan Giles
for the part they played in the writing
of this book. Their many corrections and
suggestions have made it much
clearer and easier to read.

Biblical Abbreviations

OLD TESTAMENT

Genesis	Gn	Nehemiah	Ne	Baruch	Ba
Exodus	Ex	Tobit	Tb	Ezekiel	Ezk
Leviticus	Lv	Judith	Jdt	Daniel	Dn
Numbers	Nb	Esther	Est	Hosea	Ho
Deuteronomy	Dt	1 Maccabees	1 M	Joel	Jl
Joshua	Jos	2 Maccabees	2 M	Amos	Am
Judges	Jg	Job	Jb	Obadiah	Ob
Ruth	Rt	Psalms	Ps	Jonah	Jon
1 Samuel	1 S	Proverbs	Pr	Micah	Mi
2 Samuel	2 S	Ecclesiastes	Ec	Nahum	Na
1 Kings	1 K	Song of Songs	Sg	Habakkuk	Hab
2 Kings	2 K	Wisdom	Ws	Zephaniah	Zp
1 Chronicles	1 Ch	Sirach	Si	Haggai	Hg
2 Chronicles	2 Ch	Isaiah	Is	Malachi	Ml
Ezra	Ezr	Jeremiah	Jr	Zechariah	Zc
		Lamentations	Lm		

NEW TESTAMENT

Matthew	Mt	Ephesians	Ep	Hebrews	Heb
Mark	Mk	Philippians	Ph	James	Jm
Luke	Lk	Colossians	Col	1 Peter	1 P
John	Jn	1 Thessalonians	1 Th	2 Peter	2 P
Acts	Ac	2 Thessalonians	2 Th	1 John	1 Jn
Romans	Rm	1 Timothy	1 Tm	2 John	2 Jn
1 Corinthians	1 Cor	2 Timothy	2 Tm	3 John	3 Jn
2 Corinthians	2 Cor	Titus	Tt	Jude	Jude
Galatians	Gal	Philemon	Phm	Revelation	Rv

Contents

Acknowledgments v

Biblical Abbreviations.. vi

Introduction.. ix

Chapter 1:   Paul's Background...............................1

Chapter 2:   Paul's Faith-Convictions.........................9

Chapter 3:   Faith: A Loving Response to God 19

Chapter 4:   Seeking God's Will 25

Chapter 5:   The Will and the Feelings...................... 33

Chapter 6:   The Passion in Our Lives 47

Chapter 7:   The Passion in Prayer..........................55

Chapter 8:   The Holy Spirit 65

Chapter 9:   Personal Prayer 73

Chapter 10:   The Bosom of God 77

Chapter 11:   Recollection 83

Chapter 12:   Penances....................................91

Chapter 13:   Other Spiritual Helps 97

Chapter 14:   Role of the Director 105

Chapter 15:   Mystical Death 113

Chapter 16:   Death and Detachment 121

Chapter 17:   Mystical Nativity and Spiritual Childhood .. 129

Chapter 18:   Relating to Others 133

Chapter 19:   The Fruits of a Life of Prayer 143

Introduction

In this latter part of the 20th century, much is being written and done concerning spiritual direction in the United States, and indeed throughout the rest of the English-speaking world. Many people are devoting themselves to a more intense life of prayer and imitation of Jesus. Those who do so find themselves in need of help. Like the Hebrews of old, they are journeying through a desert and look for someone to guide them. Those who are asked to be guides, however, are often fearful. "Who will guide us?" they ask. Thank God we have had in the tradition of our Church men and women who have been highly successful directors in the past and have left us their own ways of leading those who sought to live to the full, the life of Jesus within them.

St. Paul of the Cross was just such a guide. A saint and a mystic, and founder of the Passionist Fathers and Brothers, and their female counterparts, the Passionist Nuns, he has left us a rich legacy of spiritual direction. This legacy, however, is not well known. Unlike St. John of the Cross, the great Spanish Carmelite mystic of the sixteenth century, Paul did not write books on the interior life or become a Doctor of the Church. Unlike St. Ignatius of Loyola, another great spiritual director, Paul did not leave us a detailed plan of Spiritual Exercises. For this reason, his approach to spiritual direction is largely unknown, especially outside of Europe.

Paul did not write books, but he did write letters, mostly of spiritual direction. Fortunately, many of these letters have been preserved. More than two thousand have been discovered to date, and more may yet be found, since it has been estimated that he wrote over ten thousand letters in his lifetime. One reason most of them have been lost is that Paul often asked those to whom he wrote to destroy them after reading them. We know, for example, that he wrote some 500 letters of spiritual direction to Rosa Calabresi, and then told her to burn them before he died. Presumably she did, since we have none of them today.

From the rich gold mine of the letters that have been preserved we can draw many treasures. Paul's words are full of light and help for those who are groping for that light and struggling for that help today as they strive to walk in the footsteps of Christ. May the Holy Spirt help those who read this book to a deeper life of faith and Christian love.

Dear Lord, you who so captivated the heart of Paul of the Cross by the outpouring of love from the pierced heart of your Son on the Cross, welcome us as well, with the same power of that love, as we walk together on our journey to you. Amen.

SPIRITUAL DIRECTION
ACCORDING TO ST. PAUL OF THE CROSS

CHAPTER I

Paul's Background

"But, General, if you fire cannonballs into the town, you will work much destruction and kill many people. Is it worth it? They will be surrendering to you in a few days anyway." So spoke Paul of the Cross to General de Las Minas, the commandant of the Spanish army besieging the town of Orbetello in what is now Italy in the year 1735. Fortunately the general listened to Paul and Paul was right. The Austrian soldiers using the city as a fortress did surrender shortly afterwards.

This little dialogue serves as an example of the turbulent times in which St. Paul of the Cross lived and worked. His life spanned most of the eighteenth century (1694-1775). During this time there were many changes in the boundaries of the states that now comprise Italy, and constant adjustments to new governments and new situations. The unrest in the British colonies was to break out in the American Revolution the year Paul died. The discontent and turbulence in France was to peak in the even more violent French Revolution in the same century. Yet, during such a time of upheaval Paul himself succeeded in finding his own peace and leading many others to find theirs.

Birth and Early Life

Paul was born on January 3, 1694 in Ovada, a little village in northern Italy, about an hour's ride today north of Genoa. His father was a merchant, dealing mostly in tobacco. The family moved about and lived in several villages in Paul's early years before settling in Castellazzo, not far from Ovada. It was there that Paul spent most of his formative years. As he grew older he worked with his father and helped support the family.

When he was 21, in response to the request of the Pope for a crusade against the Turks who were threatening that fabled city, Paul entered the army of Venice. His deeply religious spirit was at odds with army life, though, and he left after about a year. The war never did materialize, but it was another indication of the turbulent spirit of the times.

Finding his Vocation

During times of trouble, people look for peace. In Castellazzo there was a group of young men who met together regularly to share their lives and faith and pray together. They chose Paul as their leader. Gradually most of them left home to enter the priesthood or religious orders, but Paul remained at home until his late twenties to help his father support the family.

Previously Paul had had a vision in which he was told that he would found a religious order. However, it was not yet made clear to him exactly what form this order would take or how he should go about its formation. God often gives His lights by degrees and, since Paul did not know how to proceed further, he waited a few years after that first vision till God gave more indications. One such indication came near the end of the year 1720 when Paul was almost 27 years of age. At that time he came to the decision that his family no longer needed his support, so that he could proceed to the first step in following the inspirations God had given him. He asked the bishop of the diocese (Alessandria) to clothe him with the habit of a hermit until God showed him more clearly what he was to do.

On November 22, 1720 the bishop vested him with a black habit and allowed him to live in a hermitage or little room behind the main altar of the church of St. Charles in Castellazzo. There Paul made a forty-day retreat in imitation of the forty days Jesus spent in the desert before beginning His public life. During this retreat he wrote a rule of life which serves as a model for the rule by which Passionists live today. At the request of the bishop he also wrote a diary describing his mystical experiences and many of his views on prayer. From these writings, which we have today, it is easy to see how the Holy Spirit was forming his heart to become the outstanding spiritual director he was soon called on to be, leading him and developing in him the qualities necessary to become an extraordinary spiritual director, and this in the near future.

After many setbacks Paul Danei did succeed in founding the Passionist Congregation. The first monastery was completed in 1737 after seventeen years of struggle. Although the rule he wrote was first approved provisionally in 1741, it did not get its final and definitive approval from Rome until 1769. During all these years Paul lived the life of what we might call a contemplative missionary. He spent about half of his time in his own retreats (monasteries, as they are usually called), and the other half traveling from town to town giving missions in parishes and retreats to priests and Sisters.

Becoming a Spiritual Director

As a result of all these missions and retreats, Paul met many people who desired to receive spiritual direction and guidance from him. Though reluctant to engage in what he considered a sublime and spiritual activity, he was always willing to do so when the Lord would indicate it. He did provide that guidance to many people during the missions and retreats, and continued that guidance afterwards. At times he would even return to the same places precisely for that purpose. However, because travel was slow (mostly on foot), and face-to-face direction necessarily had to be rare, most people who sought Paul's guidance did so by writing to him. This is a much more difficult way to obtain guidance and much more taxing for Paul, hut it is a blessing for us today, since so many of Paul's letters of guidance have been preserved.

Paul did not keep the letters of those who wrote to him. Once he had answered them he destroyed them. He hoped that those who received his letters would do the same, but many of them did not, so many in fact that today we have over 2000 of his letters still preserved. Even this is only part of what he wrote, since it has been calculated that he wrote over 10,000 letters in his lifetime. This had to be quite a chore in the days before typewriters and word-processors when everything had to be written by hand. An English translation of his letters appeared in the year 2000.

To some people Paul wrote only once, or a few times, but to others he wrote extensively over long periods of time. For example, he wrote to Mother Mary of the Crucified, the foundress with Paul of the Passionist nuns, over a period of about 34 years, though only 32 letters are still extant. To Agnes Grazi, a young woman he directed, he wrote at least 165 letters over a period of 14 years until her early death.

To Thomas Fossi, an impulsive married man, he wrote 171 letters that we still have. Unfortunately, as we mentioned in the Introduction, the 500 or so letters he wrote to Rosa Calabresi have all been destroyed, and at Paul's own request. In some matters we might wish that she had not been so obedient to her director. We can see from the number of letters he wrote and the time spans involved that Paul was faithful to those whose direction he accepted.

Paul was also patient. For example, when Thomas Fossi thought it would be a good idea to live as brother and sister with his wife but wanted Paul's approval, Paul would not hear of the idea, as we will see in more detail later on. Thomas kept insisting on his desire for marital continence over a period of nearly 30 years, but Paul was equally insistent that such behavior was not from the Lord. If Paul did not believe in something, he was not about to agree to it, no matter how much he was pressured.

Reluctance to Direct

Paul never wanted to be a spiritual director. He had such a sense of his own unworthiness and the importance of spiritual direction that he said he was incapable of directing "even an ant" (I, 147). He told Agnes repeatedly that he did not consider himself capable of directing her. When he refused to direct her, she refused his refusal. Finally, the signs of God's will were so clear that he had to give in. At one point he wrote to her, "I have given you so many refusals about your direction because I do not believe in myself. A director ought to be a very learned man, a man of great prayer and experience. All these are wanting in me and therefore I refuse to direct... but when God wills it, through so many rebuffs, at least I cannot discontinue assisting the souls God has confided to me" (I, 177). However, even after accepting the responsibility of being her spiritual director, Paul frequently mentions his desire to be free of this responsibility.

There were others, though, whom Paul refused to direct since he did not see any signs from God that this was what He wanted. This is understandable, since unless a person is willing to give him/herself to a life of prayer and daily seeking of God, they are not yet ready for ongoing spiritual direction.

Yet Paul was deeply convinced of the need of direction for anyone who wanted to lead a deep prayer life. He himself always sought direction. He knew what it felt like to deal, not only with good spiritual directors, but with poor ones. Most of the latter Paul had experienced before he was clothed with the habit. For example, they suggested that he keep meditating on hell when he was unable to do this. They did not understand his spirit and gave him very little positive help. For most of Paul's life his director was his brother, Father John Baptist, who was his first companion as a Passionist. After John's death he selected Father John Mary Cioni, a holy Passionist, who remained Paul's director until Paul's death.

In a letter to Agnes, Paul gives us an insight into his own beautiful spirit and the need of God's guidance to be a spiritual director, "You tell me that I wish to change God's will because in directing you, I have given so many refusals. Oh, my child, if you only knew how much I want to do God's holy will in all things! All my poor prayers are directed to no other end. I seek nothing else, I long for nothing else save in all things to be transformed by love into the divine will. I pray my divine Savior to ensure that my daily bread may be to do his beloved and adorable will and to do it with the greatest perfection; for this, holiness, learning, experience, prudence and a clear call from God are needed. For this reason, not only to you but to other souls, I have given repeated refusals, conscious of my own lack of suitability, competence and my depth of imperfection. Notwithstanding this, I have had a measure of success because souls to which I have given refusals have had strong impulses and inspirations that I should assist them. To obey the divine commands, I serve them unceasingly and I will continue to do so as long as God requires it of me, even though I am most unworthy of a task so noble and divine. You must pray a lot for me so that his divine Majesty may give me much light and assistance" (I, 148).

In this letter, Paul shows the pull he had in both directions. He was so aware of the importance and sublimity of spiritual direction and his own faultiness that he shied away from it. Yet he was so totally surrendered to God's will that when there was any indication that God wanted him to direct anyone, he did it, whether for a short span or for many years.

Love for Those he Directed

Even though Paul was reluctant to accept anyone for direction, once he did begin the process, he found God giving him great love for those he directed. He speaks of this in one of his letters. "I love all souls, and especially those whom God has entrusted to me for spiritual direction. My soul experiences a completely spiritual bond which binds it more strongly to one soul, less so to another, according to the greater or lesser love to which God has called that soul. Let me explain what I mean. If one soul has reached a higher degree of love and union with God than another, then (as God has given me to understand it), I am certain that, just as that soul is more loved by the Supreme Good, so the bond of charity links my soul more closely with it. But that does not mean it is not united in charity with others also, but more with one, less with another, as the Supreme Good wishes it" (I, 149).

Paul showed this love by entering into relationship with those he was directing and sharing himself with them. The communication between them became a two-way street, even as far as Paul's sharing the depths of his personal faith and conversation with the Lord was concerned. We find Paul constantly revealing himself his concerns, anxieties, problems, longings and joys with those he directed. The relationship for him was never purely professional, but was also personal, though more deeply so with some than with others.

Sharing Himself

He wrote to Mother Mary Crucified, "Pray for me because my needs are great. Offer the Most Precious Blood of Jesus and the Sorrows of Mary to the eternal Father, and ask for assistance, help and mercy for this poor sinner who has so many troubles, which I gladly embrace for the love of Jesus Christ" (II, 290). Another time he wrote to her, "Even though I get up every day, this does not mean that I have the strength. Rather, I feel more and more depressed and exhausted. Still, I am very happy, because it pleases God" (II, 325). In the very first letter Paul wrote to her, he devoted more space to sharing his own problems than to discussing hers.

To Agnes, Paul wrote in even stronger terms, "My child in Jesus Christ, I want to let you know that your poor spiritual father is plunged into the depths of misery, both within and without. And although my soul has never been without a cross, now I am in such a state that I am stricken with horror by the great assaults and attacks of my enemies. My sins deserve this. Say nothing about this for I don't write to seek your sympathy. No indeed. It is only for you to pray and get prayers said for this most wretched of men who is now overwhelmed in the very extremity of direct need. On the outside I put on a calm face so as not to frighten anyone, for God wants me to act thus, but on the inside I am in the midst of a great stormy sea. Do you also ask the Divine Infant to bestow on me the grace that may gain me the victory" (I, 122).

These days much is written about spiritual direction being more of a peer relationship than a paternalistic one. Even though there were some signs of paternalism in Paul, such as calling Agnes, "My dear child," yet in what he wrote, Paul's sharing with those he directed was often on a peer basis. These sharings of his troubles are a clear example of peer relationship.

Often Paul shared not only his present troubles, but even his past ones. We find one example in a letter to Francis Appiani when that young man was experiencing doubts and difficulties as he considered whether or not he should become a Passionist. Paul told Francis of his own experiences at a similar time in his own life. "Oh, if you only knew the trials I myself experienced before embracing the kind of life I now lead! The devil suggested great fears to me. I was touched with compassion for my parents whom I was leaving in great poverty, and whose every hope in this world rested on me. I experienced interior desolation, depression, doubts. It seemed to me that I would never be able to persevere in my vocation. To crown my misfortune, all devotion had vanished. I felt dry and was tried in everyway. Even the sound of the church bells disturbed me. Everyone seemed happy except me!" (I, 411).

Paul did not share himself this way with everyone, but only with those to whom he related closely. In doing this he was not looking for sympathy, as he himself says, though it doubtless was a relief to him, as it would be to any of us, to share with someone who loved him. Paul had the same need to share his troubles that we all do and that even Jesus had in Gethsemane. Paul certainly was not looking for an opportunity to "dump" his troubles on someone else. But he was looking for prayer support, as he says clearly, and as Jesus did too. Jesus and Paul both felt that they could share their troubles with their closest friends. Paul did not see this sharing as in any way compromising his spiritual direction, since, as we have considered before, he never considered spiritual direction as a one-way street. Paul was always willing and ready to receive as well as to give. In this, Paul was ahead of his time.

After this brief look at Paul's life and his attitude to spiritual direction, let us now take a closer look at the way in which he went about assisting people on their journey to God.

CHAPTER 2

Paul's Faith-Convictions

aul's deep faith-convictions were the underpinning of his spiritual direction. Let us take a look at some of these faith-convictions which Paul may originally have heard or read about first from someone else, but which became his own through his personal relationship to God and his own deep prayer life.

What Faith-Convictions Are

When we speak of his faith-convictions, we are not speaking of assumptions or unthought-out opinions. Paul was open to new discoveries about the Lord all the time. But once he had come to be convinced of something, he did not keep going over it. He accepted it as a "given." He did not need to keep re-inventing the wheel. We call these opinions and convictions "faith-presuppositions," since Paul presumes them in all his spiritual direction. He assumes that those he is directing have these faith-convictions also and that it is not necessary to prove them or discuss their validity. He uses such belief to draw new conclusions and to come to greater insights into the spiritual life.

Like all of us, Paul also had his cultural presuppositions: ideas he had taken from his culture without question. Some of these were social ideas, such as the way in which men and women should relate. Some were political ideas, such as the presumptions that the governmental structure of the Church at his time was exactly as it should be. Some of them were culturally religious ideas, such as the presumption that Protestants were outside the Church. We cannot expect him or anyone else to question all the presumptions of their time, and we always need to make allowances for these, even in understanding Sacred Scripture. But Paul's faith-presuppositions were truths he derived from his own personal experience of God and what God was like. Let us take a look at a few of them.

God's Power

1. God is all-powerful. However, his power is always directed by his love. All events in the world are willed and controlled by him and he brings them to good for those who love him (Rm 8:28). Even suffering is totally under God's control and he never lets us experience even one drop of it more than is necessary. God is all-powerful. There is no other person or force outside of God's control who is bringing about suffering or anything else. God is in control of everything, even though he allows other persons or inanimate creatures, such as the weather, to have their effect on our lives too.

Most of the things that happen to us are evidently good. Our tendency is to ascribe to God only those things that look good to us instead of believing that all things are from God whether they look good to us or not. We need God's own light to see and be convinced that all things are from him. If they don't seem good to us at present, he will eventually bring them to good even in our eyes. However, sometimes the final chapter is written only in eternity, as it was for Jesus. We need to learn to trust that God knows what he is doing and will bring all to good, even though many things will not appear this way to us until eternity. It was the attitude of Jesus towards such apparent evils that Paul tried to develop in those he directed. Take these words of Paul as an example: "Do not be disturbed by the passing trials you are going through, since you must know that similar trials will come often. Our divine Savior visits those servants who are dear to him and purifies them with trials to develop their fidelity" (II, 489). And again, "The words of God always meet with opposition so that the divine magnificence may shine forth. It is when things appear to be crashing to the ground that you will see them even more be raised on high. 'The Lord has dominion over life and death. He leads down to the gates of the nether world and leads back [Ws 16:13]'" (I, 86).

Creatures are God's Instruments

Paul considers creatures, whether human or otherwise, simply as God's instruments even when we suffer from them. He has this advice: "Take the trials you suffer, whether in body or in spirit, also any other storm which arises from men or devils, and all the desolation, abandonment, darkness, temptation, and so forth, take them all, I say, without any intermediary, from the most gentle heart of Jesus" (I, 620). And again, "Look at your trials with the eye of faith, not as coming from creatures, hut from the loving hand of God" (I, 624). We have already mentioned that Paul does not try to prove his faith-presuppositions, but presumes that those he directs will understand them and accept them. Paul does not try to prove that God is all-powerful and directs all things. What Paul would do if individuals wanted his direction, but did not believe this about God, is hard to say. Probably Paul would try to show them from the Scriptures that God's loving providence directs all things. If they still did not believe what he was saying, Paul would probably not go on with the guidance. Paul's whole direction presumes that no one apart from God is in control of our lives or any part of them.

Where Free Will Comes In

"But what of free will?" someone might ask. This is a very deep question, which has mystified theologians for centuries. "How can we believe that God directs all things and yet that we have free will?" That God directs all things is a clear teaching of our faith and well attested to in Sacred Scripture. The Bible has many references to God's all-powerful guidance of his creation, but perhaps none more extensive than the final chapters of the Book of Job. Also the Epistle to the Ephesians tells us, in a very mysterious statement, "We are God's handiwork, created in Christ Jesus for the purpose of carrying out those good works which God has prepared beforehand" (2:10).

At the same time, human freedom is clearly proclaimed in Scripture, especially when Jesus tells us, "You will know the truth and the truth will set you free" (Jn 8:32). Paul of the Cross believed in human freedom, "Always leave yourself in holy freedom" (I, 580), he writes. But Paul was not a speculative theologian, and never tried to go into the problem of how human freedom and divine causality fit together. He simply accepted both and never tried to fathom the mystery of how these two truths relate. He well knew, of course that theologians had never been able to clarify this mystery even after centuries of groping with it. So he had the common sense to leave

11

it alone. He firmly believed that God directs all things and also that God gives us our freedom. He never tried to reconcile these two statements. Paul was not interested in academic questions anyway. He was comfortable with mystery and could leave unsolvable mysteries alone. He presumed that those he directed would leave them alone too. He was a practical man and his interest was to lead people to God.

God ~ Constant Activity

2. A second faith-conviction of Paul which he presumes in all his direction was this: God is actively doing something in our hearts at every moment and is communicating with us at every moment. As the Scriptures put it, "He neither slumbers nor sleeps, the guardian of Israel" (Ps 121:4). The popular Psalm 139 has an even longer and more poetic expression of this truth:

> Lord, you have probed me and you know me;
> you know when I sit and when I stand;
> you understand my thoughts from afar.
> My journeys and my rest you scrutinize,
> with all my ways you are familiar.
> Even before a word is on my tongue,
> behold, O Lord, you know the whole of it.
> Behind me and before, you hem me in
> and rest your hand upon me.

As long as we are not positively resisting this activity or refusing to listen to God's communication, we are picking it up in the center of our being, even though not always on the conscious level. This too is a truth that Paul never tries to prove but just presumes for those he directs.

He writes, "Remain in the divine presence in everything you do. If you are busy at work with your hands, let your mind and heart be inwardly on God" (I, 75). And again, "Be at peace in your sufferings without trying too hard to understand them in your mind. A true servant of God is praying always. I don't mean kneeling down, but with loving attention to the divine presence. Insofar as this involves a lack of feeling of God's presence, so much the better" (I, 547).

Paul's Idea of Prayer

When Paul speaks of prayer, he never means simply talking to God and then presuming, as so many do today, that God never speaks to them, but only to certain chosen souls. Paul believed that all true prayer is a two-way street and that God is always communicating to the hearts of those who will listen. He writes, "Prayer can go on continuously with a loving gaze on God in pure faith, marveling at his goodness, his greatness, or just who he is" (I, 549).

Paul does not try to prove this activity either. He simply expresses his own faith-conviction that God is always trying to communicate with us. Most people think they are praying (communicating with God) only when they consciously initiate it. They don't expect God to speak to them. Paul teaches those he directs to be attentive to God in the silence of their hearts at all times.

Constant Prayer

Paul speaks of this constant prayer even in the midst of activity when he writes, "Do the things you have to do. Work diligently, but with peace of heart and a quiet spirit, remaining in the presence of God. With your hands, work; with your heart, treat with God" (II, 19). He is a bit more detailed when he says, "Prayer should be continuous, waking and sleeping, walking and standing, working and resting. Such prayer is made in the deepest part of the sacred interior desert, in deepest solitude, in loving interior repose in God, totally absorbed and lost in that sea of infinite love" (II, 292). It was because Paul believed that God was always communicating, that he could recommend such constant inner attention to God in the depths of the heart even in the midst of a busy day.

Paul was deeply desirous that those he directed should keep themselves in a spirit of open responsiveness to what God was saying. This openness was in the heart. The mind had to be occupied with the task of the moment, but the inner willingness for whatever God might want was in the heart. As Paul puts it in another letter, "When we remain with a loving attention of heart on God in living faith, we pray twenty four hours a day. This is because we become accustomed to remain interiorly always in the presence of God, adoring him in spirit and in truth [Jn 4:24]. Let that precious desire saturate everything and penetrate even to the marrow of your bones" (I, 443).

Most people presume that it is necessary to be aware that they are praying in order to pray. There is an old saying among the spiritual masters that if you are aware you are praying, you are not praying very deeply. Paul would certainly have agreed with that. For him, the important thing was not conscious awareness, but openness of heart to God's will. In situations where our will is one with God's, we are often not even aware of praying. It is when we are starting to resist his will or deviate from it that we become aware of it.

Openness to God's will is like having a telephone in the house. As long as we are not doing anything that makes a deafening noise, like vacuuming a rug, we will probably hear the phone if it rings. But we do not have to think of the telephone at all times. In fact, we usually don't think of it at all unless it rings. That is the way it needs to be with God. We need to be ready for any indication of what he wants of us. But if we are busy doing the work God gives us to do, we will have our minds focused on that work and won't even think of God. We don't need to. Our hearts are on him already and that is the important thing. We are inwardly praying, even though we are not conscious of it. Paul believed that God is always speaking to us in the deep inner silence of our hearts and as long as we are willing for what he wants or might want of us, then we are hearing his voice and we are praying.

We Hear God's Love through the Passion

3. A third faith-conviction of Paul which he presumes his readers will understand and believe is this: The Passion of Jesus is the greatest work and sign of God's love. He constantly repeats this in different ways in his letters of direction and would never dream of trying to prove it. It is a "given" for Paul and underlies his whole approach to prayer. Paul thinks of the Passion, though, not merely as a past event, but as a present sign which we need to contemplate and allow to penetrate us. Paul often thinks of the Passion and its past details as he knew them from the Scriptures and encourages those he directs to do the same. But he does not want them to stay in the past. He wants them to see the Passion as a present sign of God's love.

Paul never focuses on the Passion in a merely negative way, looking only at the pain, tears, blood and dirt, but Paul looked deeper than the wounds of Jesus to see the love beneath the wounds. Each event and each wound had for Paul its own particular significance. It was a sign of some love-attitude in the heart of Christ. Walking in the footsteps of Jesus meant for Paul imitating the love-attitudes of the heart of Jesus which he saw in the Passion; the virtues and values of Jesus: the humility, courage, patience, confidence, compassion for others, obedience to the Father and many other virtues. Here are some examples of what the Passion meant for Paul.

"The world lives unmindful of the sufferings of Jesus which are the miracle of miracles of the love of God. We must arouse the world from its slumber. His Holy Spirit will teach us how" (II, 726). And also, "God can work in us only when we pass through the door which is Jesus Christ and his most holy Passion, which is the greatest and most stupendous work of his love" (II, 499).

All is From God's Love

Paul could never consider the Passion of Jesus or any suffering apart from the love of God. He never saw it as some, for example, would say, "Why is that terrible thing happening?" Or, "God does not want this to happen. He loves us." Or, "If he loves us, how can he allow this terrible thing to happen?" Even though Paul could feel the pain of his own sufferings and be compassionate towards others in their sufferings, yet he immediately saw them as part of the Passion and encouraged those he directed to do the same. He wrote to Agnes Grazi of his own sufferings and connected them with the Passion of Jesus. He said he was "totally immersed in that bottomless abyss of divine love and in the red sea of the most holy Passion of Jesus. This sea comes from the infinite love of God" (I, 267). Paul would never ask the question, "Why is God doing this to me?" He saw that whatever was happening to him was a share in what the Father asked of Jesus. In some mysterious way, it was all love and led to love, even though the particular why of it was and will always remain a mystery.

Paul could break forth into raptures considering God's love which he found in the Passion. He writes to Agnes, "Have courage, Agnes, that God will complete the work he has begun. Let the poor butterfly be totally burned and incinerated in the most sweet furnace of the loving heart of Jesus. Then let the few ashes of our nothingness be buried, be lost, be consumed in that abyss of the infinite love of our God. There, melted down in love, make a continuous feast, with loving songs, with holy enjoyment, with dreams of love, with holy silence, all absorbed in that immense sea of love. In this sea, swim to the depths and there you will find another great sea of the sufferings of Jesus and the sorrows of Mary most holy. This sea flows forth from the immense sea of God's love. Oh, what a wonder this is!" (I, 280).

The Passion: a Wellspring of Virtue and Power

Paul also looked at the Passion as the source of all the virtues we need to practice as we walk in the footsteps of Jesus. He writes to Lucy Burlini, another mystic whom he guided for years, "I recommend that you go often in spirit to fish in the most holy sea of the sufferings of Jesus Christ and the sorrows of Mary most holy. In this great sea you will fish up the jewels of the holy virtues of our sweet Jesus and your soul will become always more beautiful as it is adorned with these precious gems" (II, 717).

Paul not only looked at the various events of the Passion to see the virtues of Christ, he found the power to act the way Jesus did in that same contemplation. Paul found also the power not only to act with the various virtues of Christ, but also to purify his faults. As he wrote to Agnes, "Cast yourself into the loving furnace of the Passion so that all the mold of your imperfections will be burned away and you will become a pure bread for the table of the King of glory" (I, 229).

Our Sufferings and the Passion

Paul connects all sufferings with the Passion, not only pain and distress but everything we do not naturally like. To make this connection, Paul looked at the different sufferings that Jesus not only endured, but accepted during his Passion: inner anguish, terrible fear and depression, abandonment by his friends, betrayal, deprivation of his freedom, injustice, lies told about him, excommunication, rejection by authority, especially by religious authority, bodily pain, utter fatigue, misunderstanding, helplessness, a sense of failure, the feeling of being abandoned by his Father, and finally death itself. From his own long meditations, Paul had all these sufferings of Jesus to draw on when he made parallels for others and asked them to choose for themselves what Jesus had chosen for himself.

In one letter, or really many letters, but in this one in particular, he connects dryness in prayer with the Passion. Writing to Theresa Palozzi, a young lady who later became a Passionist nun, he says, "It is a good sign that you suffer dryness in prayer. By means of this, God purifies you like gold in the furnace, and makes your soul pure and beautiful in his divine eyes. Make frequent acts of acceptance of the will of God, embrace it on the cross of Jesus, and remain crucified with him, suffering whatever his divine majesty arranges in a silence of faith and holy love" (III, 363).

Paul not only connects sufferings with the Passion, but calls them "love-gifts." "Sufferings are the most precious gifts that God is accustomed to share with those souls who are most dear to him. Embrace them with acceptance as coming from the most loving heart of Jesus Christ. Suffer your afflictions in silence to exercise that holy patience which includes within itself works which are perfect" (II, 30).

It was with these faith-convictions that Paul approached the spiritual direction of those who came to him for help: God is all powerful, all-loving, and directs all the events of our lives by his love, while preserving and even causing our freedom; he is constantly communicating with us to the full extent of our willingness to be open to his will; and he sent his Son to suffer and die for us as the greatest sign he has ever given of the extent of his love. Let us now see how Paul carried out this direction in practice.

CHAPTER 3

Faith: A Loving Response to God

The primary attitude Paul looked for in those he directed was faith. As he wrote to Mother Mary Crucified, "Dark faith is the sure guide of holy love" (II, 289). By faith, Paul did not mean what is often called faith today, namely the intellectual assent to propositions, like "I believe in the communion of saints." For Paul, faith was an action that involved the whole person, a complete surrender to God to be led by his Holy Spirit in everything. It was a total capitulation to a loving God, allowing and desiring him to direct our lives. This is really the gospel and biblical meaning of faith. Much Catholic teaching has tended to limit faith to an acceptance with the mind of a body of truths rather than the total surrender of the person to God. Paul, for example, gives this piece of advice, "When you, stripped of everything, gently feel yourself on the cross, stir up your faith in God's presence, and abandon yourself in the immense sea of his love" (I, 140). Without such faith, Paul did not believe it possible to begin any journey into a deep prayer life, a life of communication with the Lord. He had many things to say about inner peace, not being deceived, and so forth, as we will see later on, but when we are trying to understand what he means in the advice he is giving, we have to remember that he is giving it to persons who have made a faith commitment to Jesus. His words would not fit anyone else. What Paul has to say about the place of suffering in our lives, for example, will seem like utter foolishness to anyone who has not made this faith-commitment.

Paul identified faith with a loving desire to please God in everything. He writes again, "The just person lives by faith. The lover does not seek any happiness other than to please God" (I, 129). Paul sees this faith, not as a cold intellectual exercise, but as the constant condition of one who has come to love God ardently, always seeking ways to please him.

Faith Transforms

Paul saw faith as a transforming power, not only enabling us to know and do what pleases God, but changing our own hearts in the bargain. He expresses it this way, "As you are crucified with Christ, you become more and more transformed in God through faith and love" (II, 719). He writes to Agnes, "Every effort should be made to pray in pure and living faith, to seek God alone, to live in him, to languish with love for him, to remain at rest in his divine Majesty" (I, 165). Also, "I don't want you to be uneasy about anything that happens in prayer, but in everything be at one with what pleases God. Oh, how I rejoice that prayer is made in faith! This is the loving way in which God has always inspired me to direct you" (I, 1698).

Our Guide is Faith, not Feelings

Paul speaks of faith as a guide of prayer, and the way to avoid deception. He says, "The certain way is holy faith, making your prayer with a faith that is alive, with a continual remembrance of the Passion of Jesus" (I, 443). He often repeats this advice in his letters, frequently referring to the great Carmelite mystic, St. John of the Cross as a guide in this matter. John of the Cross has beautiful mystical poetry in which he calls faith the sure guide in the dark night of our journey.

Both Paul of the Cross and John of the Cross are most emphatic in insisting that we trust our faith. The human tendency is to go by our feelings. Often when people begin the inner journey in the footsteps of Jesus, there are many uplifting feelings that God gives. But these are like milk given to a baby and God gradually weans them from these feelings. We have a good example of this in the Gospel in the account of the transfiguration (Lk 9:28-36). While Jesus was praying, along with Peter, James, and John, Peter asked him if they could build three shacks to camp there and continue to bask in the exhilaration they were feeling. He was on cloud nine and did not want to fall off. But the dark cloud, which is a symbol of faith, soon overshadowed them, as it does all who seek to lead a life of prayer. That is when many get scared as Peter did and need reassurance that things are all right.

Paul of the Cross assured those he directed that when the original feelings go, it is all right just to let them go. Don't struggle to get them back. It is faith which is our guide, not our feelings. In fact, it is dangerous to try to guide our life by feelings, since they are so changeable and deceptive. Paul had to repeat his advice on many occasions, since those he directed and all of us have the tendency to judge our prayer by the way we feel instead of trusting God in the darkness of faith, even though we feel nothing.

Faith Sees God in Events

It is faith which allows us to see God's hand in events and to hear his voice through them. Paul speaks of this function of faith, and in this he is reflecting another of his mentors, St. Francis de Sales, whose books he loved to read. Paul advises this approach, "Look at events as coming from the loving heart of our sweet Jesus, who allows them for our spiritual profit" (II, 357). We have already spoken of Paul's attitude towards suffering as something purposeful in God's hands and not something that is simply indifferent or even evil and in which God has no part. It is faith which enables us to see God's hand in events even when humanly we cannot understand them.

When we see them as acts of his love, then they are messages of his love and look for a response from us. As our heart responds with acceptance, even though this may be painful at times, it is praying, even though we may not feel that we are praying at all. This is one aspect of the constant communication with God that Paul the apostle speaks of ("Pray always" [1 Th 5:17]), and which Paul of the Cross constantly encouraged. He never saw prayer as limited to the times when we can focus our minds on God, but an activity for the whole day, as we listen in our spirit for God's messages of love. We looked at Paul's recommendations in regard to this kind of prayer in the last chapter. Of course, Paul has much to say of the prayer in which we take time to focus on the Lord during the day and we will have more to say about that later.

Freedom from Other's Opinions

In addition to letting our feelings control our judgments and our actions, another obstacle to prayer is letting others have undue influence on us. We are too often concerned about what others are saying or thinking of us. I once saw a little maxim in a magazine which went something like this, "We would be much less concerned with what others are thinking of us if we only knew how rarely they do." For Paul, what others might be thinking was irrelevant. The only thing we need be concerned with is what we hear the Lord indicating as we catch it in our hearts through faith. One way he puts it is this: "Always be obedient to the inner indications and attractions the Holy Spirit gives you. Jesus desires a complete detachment from all that is created, a true mystical death to all that is not God, and a great nakedness and poverty of spirit in order to be completely clothed with the most pure faith and love for Jesus Christ" (II, 717). Incidentally, the expression, "death to all that is not God," which Paul frequently uses, comes from another of his favorite authors, the medieval German Dominican mystic, John Tauler. St. John of the Cross, who wrote two centuries after Tauler, also uses it.

As long as we are attached to our desire for the approval of others, we will find it difficult to hear the voice of God in faith. For example, suppose someone hurts us. Jesus' voice, which we hear through our faith, tells us to forgive even seventy times seven (Mt 18:22). But our culture would not tell us that. Did you ever see a John Wayne or Clint Eastwood movie in which either forgave the villain at the end? Others would tell us to get even and would consider forgiving as absolutely crazy. If these others happen to be persons with whom we live or work it can he hard to hear the words of Jesus about forgiveness. We hear him only in faith. However, if we want to follow him, we have to let his attitudes gradually become our own. No matter what the attitudes of others are, we need to listen to the voice of God in the stillness of our heart. Paul expresses it this way, "What does it matter to you what people say and that they disapprove what you are doing? Seek to please God alone and let them say what they want" (II, 295). Our spiritual receivers must be tuned in, not to our feelings, nor to the opinions of others, but to our faith.

Faith: a Gradual Response

Faith is also the way we respond to what he hear God saying to us. It is our surrender to let our lives be guided by his Spirit. Only with this surrender can there be any prayer life in depth. This is why Paul is constantly referring to faith as the guide of our inner journey with Jesus.

However, we do need patience with ourselves. It is only gradually that the Holy Spirit overcomes in us the fear of going against our feelings or the opinions of others. The whole journey is a lifelong process. But we are journeying with Jesus. He, too, had to overcome his own fears, as the Gethsemane mystery shows us, and also the disapproval of others. He had to face the disapproval of his family (Mk 3:21), the disapproval of his peers (Mt 16:22), and the disapproval of authority (Mt 21:23-27). He will enable us to have the same courage that he did and eventually to be able to walk surely in the darkness of faith without being influenced by either ourselves or others. Paul of the Cross understood how difficult the journey is, so he was constantly encouraging those he directed to walk in faith and reassuring them that they were on the right road when they had their doubts. God is always with us.

CHAPTER 4

Seeking God's Will

aving embarked on the journey of faith we need to know how to find the path at all times. For Paul faith was a certain and secure guide as we have already seen. But we know we are on the path of faith when we are seeking to know and do God's holy will. Paul himself sought to discern God's will in every situation in his life and he counseled all those he directed to do the same.

The awareness that we should accept and follow God's will is common to all Christians. We all say, "Thy will be done," in the Our Father. However, for many this means following an inflexible, iron rule of things: laws and rules and regulations and directions from authority, which often seem inhuman and heartless. The same is true of natural disasters, which seem to be utterly indifferent to human suffering. Some do not accept these as God's will, but even those who do usually have a problem with acceptance. There are probably very few who say the "Thy will be done" of the Our Father with any real enthusiasm. But Paul was one of those few. The reason he could be enthusiastic about God's will, no matter what it entailed was that in faith, he saw God's will, not as some iron rule, but as all love.

God is love, as the Scriptures tell us (1 Jn 4:16). Therefore, his will has to be all love, even when we do not recognize it as love. Paul wrote to Mother Mary Crucified, "Be faithful to God, accepting every trial from his loving hand in silence" (II, 295). When we say, "God's loving hand," it certainly is a more attractive image than when we say "God's will." Paul accustomed himself to see God's will in that attractive way and he taught those he directed to do the same.

God's Will in Events

Paul never forgot that God is all-powerful, as we have already seen. Therefore, God's will was shown for him through all events that happen, since they are all controlled by his loving providence. As Paul put it, reflecting the theology on this point he had drawn from St. Francis de Sales, "The will of God, called the will of good-pleasure by the Fathers of the Church, is known by the events which happen. Therefore, the loving soul remains calm no matter what happens (except for sin). Its food is the will of God as Jesus himself said [Jn 4:34]" (I, 292). These words of Jesus were favorite ones of Paul and are often repeated in his letters of direction. They expressed something basic to all direction, which was to see all events as coming from God's will. For Paul, this was God's love.

We usually think of accepting God's will when something unpleasant comes along and perhaps pray for inner strength to accept it. However, God's will for us is by no means all unpleasantness and suffering. Most of what God wants of us each day is very easy and enjoyable and at times even delightful. It is true, though, that we usually have more trouble accepting God's will when it is something we don't naturally like. That is why more of Paul's counsels on accepting God's will concern accepting it when it goes against our natural preferences.

Paul writes to Mother Mary Crucified, "Seek no other consolation than to please God and to do his holy will. This will is better fulfilled in aridities, desolations, abandonment and other trials than in consolations, in which even a little child is brave" (II, 295). Actually we need God's help to accept his will even when it is easy, but it is not often that we think of this need. In adversity, we immediately become aware of our own inadequacy and perhaps this is one reason why God sends adversity.

Paul accepted the will of God in everything. But, lest it seem that he lived in an unfeeling world and was encouraging those he directed to insensitivity, let us look at another statement of his when he heard of the danger that the whole Passionist congregation might be wiped out by the authorities in Rome: "I immediately abandoned myself into the arms of the Lord, adoring his divine judgments and being resolved to do his most holy will even better." Great! But then he adds the human element, "Believe me, though, the body makes itself felt and I had trouble sleeping last night" (II, 463).

God's Will in Troubles

At times, Paul specified certain types of trouble we need to accept, especially when the one he was directing was going through that particular trial. For example, most of us don't like it when our plans have to be changed and we do not readily see that change as God's will. All we see is an inconvenience to ourselves. Paul did not see it that way. Take this example from an incident in his own life. "This morning I decided to leave for Viterbo. As soon as I made the decision, I began to lose time here and there. I was to leave to go as far as Montalto in a little ship, but the wind was against us so we couldn't leave. I adore the divine will" (I, 136). Today he might say that the plane couldn't take off because of ice on the runway, which God put there with full awareness of the needs of all concerned.

Another experience we all have from time to time in which it is difficult to accept God's will is sickness. It is not just that in sickness we frequently have acute bodily pain, but that we often have to let go of the things we usually do and want to do each day, and to accept the slowness of convalescence. Paul had the same experience often and draws on it for the sake of those he directed. "I have been up now for four days with the help of one of the Religious and a cane. I walked a little bit down the corridor but then I could not hold myself up, I was so weak. I was more tired after this little walk than I used to be after walking thirty miles. But I am content with the most holy will of God" (II, 463).

Sickness often provides the occasion, not just of passively accepting the discomforts and pains we cannot prevent, but of actively doing things we would prefer not to do in the healing process, such as Paul's walking down the corridor when he doubtless would have preferred to remain sitting in his own room.

Another trial Paul speaks of is the trial of accepting an uncertain future. He speaks of it especially in connection with the possibility of a change of residence. Since this is a frequent cross in our present-day nomadic world, let us hear what Paul says on this point. "Believe me, I am an exile with no set place to live. My place and my repose is the most gentle will of my God. If God wants me here, I stay here. But if he wants me elsewhere, I will do his most holy will. As far as I can see, God wants me here for now. May he be blessed" (I, 157). There are many today who would prefer to move from where they live, but cannot because of economic limitations. There are also many who would prefer to stay where they are, but have to move for economic reasons. The grace of God is needed to accept these trials from his loving hand as purposeful and as leading to something good.

Readiness for God's Will

Paul wanted to be sure that those he directed would connect God's will not only with adversity, but with whatever, so he counsels readiness for anything. "I want to ready myself for whatever may happen and I resign and abandon myself to God's good pleasure. If he wants my work done, fine. If he wants it undone, let it be as he wills it" (II, 290).

Paul counseled being ready in advance for the cross. Whenever a particular cross comes to our minds as a possibility it is wise to accept it as soon as we can, but as a possibility. We cannot accept it as a reality, since it has not happened yet, and most things like that never do happen. But if we refuse it, or try to put it out of our minds without accepting it as a possibility, we have already resisted God's will. How often have we said or heard others say after an unpleasant happening, "I hope that never happens again." It is only natural to feel that way, but unless we can also turn to God and accept the possibility that this situation may happen again, we are already resisting God's will, and we don't even notice it. We need to be ready for the "whatever," not having our hearts closed to any possibility that occurs to us. When we have this attitude, it is so much easier to accept crosses when they actually do come.

God's Will in Pleasure and Pain

We might think that it is not necessary to speak of acceptance of God's will in what is pleasant, since we are naturally inclined to the pleasant anyway. But it is a not infrequent temptation to be slow to enter into something enjoyable for fear that we may have to "pay" for it afterwards with something painful. Paul did not have that attitude at all, nor did he counsel such an attitude. He was able to enjoy himself and wanted others to do so as well. In this, he was of the same mentality as St. Teresa of Avila, whom he read and admired very much. She put it very succinctly when she said, "When I pray, I pray; when I eat, I eat."

Paul expresses this open attitude towards God's will when he says, "Persevere in total abandonment to the divine good pleasure without examining to see whether it is painful or joyful. Let your contentment be to please God, nourishing yourself more and more on his holy will" (II, 473). He also puts it this way, "The best road to follow is to live your life entirely surrendered to God's will, as much in prosperity as in adversity. Take everything from the hand of God with a humble and peaceful spirit" (I, 672).

To Sister Columba Gandolfi he writes, "My whole point is that you should be strong with the grace of God in persevering in total abandonment to the divine good pleasure, without considering whether it is painful or pleasurable, hut that your contentment is the contentment of the Most High, as you nourish yourself always more on his most holy will" (II,473). Paul knew that we need a mixture of joy and sorrow, pleasure and pain, the easy and the difficult in life. His idea was to leave all in the hands of God and his love will blend all these as each one of us needs them. We may have trouble accepting the painful things we can't understand and which seem foolish to us, and on the other hand, we may have guilt feelings at times if things seem too easy and pleasurable. But Paul wanted those he directed to simply abandon themselves to God's will and trust him for the "whatever."

God Helps Us

However, we do not do this alone and unaided. God knows our weakness well, so he does not ask us to face adversity without help. This help he promises and it is all-powerful. Paul urges us to look for this help and to expect it. God never asks too much of us. As Paul writes to Sister Girolama Ercolani, "We need great acceptance of the most holy will of God in all our troubles. He arranges all things for our greater good and he also knows how to give his own consolation when we are least expecting it" (II, 589).

Resistance to God's Will

Our own acceptance of God's will opens us to more of God's help to make any difficult situation easier. As Paul puts it to John Francis Sancez, a young man of Orbetello he was directing, "I see you have eased so deep a wound by the most precious balm of resignation to the divine will" (II, 372) . For Paul it is our resistance to God's will that causes most of the pain. As we surrender to it more and more, the pain eases and what God is asking of us can become not only easier, but even enjoyable. It is not what God is asking of us, but our resistance to it that is the chief problem.

We might compare our resistance to God's will in a modern comparison by looking at the way different kinds of electric wires transmit or resist the current. Let us compare the electricity to God's power and the wires to our will. All wires are not the same. The wires in an electric toaster are made to resist the current and generate heat. The wires in a light cord are made to conduct the current as best as possible and they do not generate heat unless there is something wrong with them. Our own wills are like that. When we resist God's will, we get hot and feel the pain. As we surrender more and more to God's will, the wire of our will cools and there is less and less pain, or perhaps we might say that our pain is felt less and less as pain.

But how do we resist God's will? Let us take a look at Jesus, who could say, "I have come not to do my own will, but the will of him who sent me" (Jn 6:38). When Jesus spoke to his disciples about his forthcoming Passion and death, he was telling them, "It should be this way." But Peter and the rest were saying to him, "It should not be this way" instead of, "Lord, for some mysterious reason I can't understand; it should be this way, but give me the grace to accept it." As we learn to say "Yes" to the events of our lives and to the indications the Holy Spirit gives us for what he wants us to do, our inner wires resist the current less and less and more and more of God's power, peace and joy flow into us, even as we go through this or that aspect of our own Passion. The cross becomes lighter and even joyful, as it eventually did to the apostles much later in their lives when they could leave the presence of the Sanhedrin after being scourged for speaking in the name of Jesus. Scripture tells us, "They left the Sanhedrin, rejoicing that they had been found worthy to suffer dishonor for the sake of Jesus" (Ac 5:41). No one can rejoice in disgrace without the special power of the Holy Spirit. This same power is offered to us in proportion to our openness and readiness for God's will.

Degrees of Acceptance

We usually come to accept God's will the way the apostles did — by degrees. Paul speaks of these degrees: "It is great perfection to be resigned in everything to the divine will. It is greater perfection to live abandoned to the divine good pleasure, being ready for whatever comes. It is the greatest and highest perfection to nourish oneself in a pure spirit of faith and love on the divine will" (I, 491).

God could bring about in us a total and instantaneous surrender to his will so that we would be ready for heaven in a moment. Probably that is what he did to the good thief on the cross. But ordinarily he chooses to take time and allow us to move at our own pace. We need patience with ourselves as we only gradually surrender to his will, even though deep down we would doubtless prefer to surrender everything immediately. We all have rebellious feelings which cause us many problems. Paul frequently writes of the difference between our will and our feelings, as we will consider in the next chapter.

CHAPTER 5

The Will and the Feelings

When we speak of our will, we usually speak of our power of free choice, which is at the center of our being. It is with this will of free choice that we love. But often we use the word "will" to speak of our natural preference, such as Jesus did in Gethsemane when he said to his Father, "Not my will, but yours be done" (Mk 14:26). We are aware of our will of natural preference through our feelings, which go along with this will. Even when we choose to go against our feelings, we all know how hard it is, so that we can easily identify with the words of Jesus to his Father. We can also understand the struggle Paul the apostle describes in himself in the seventh chapter of the Letter to the Romans when he chose to go against this natural pull of his feelings within him.

The problem comes from the fact that our feelings have been programmed in the opposite direction to God's will and God's love since we were born. We are naturally inclined to put our own will, our own preferences, first and not prefer what God would want of us. Our natural inclination is to be selfish, not loving. As we surrender more and more deeply to Jesus and to the working of his Spirit within us, we become more and more free of the drag of our feelings. But it helps to understand the conflict in which we are engaged and how best to act in it.

It is good to remember that our choice and acceptance of God's will does not depend on our feelings. We can accept God's will by free choice, even though we don't feel like it at all, and perhaps don't even feel that we are actually accepting it. So many good people say, "I don't even want God's will," and fill themselves with guilt feelings because of this. What they really should be saying is, "I don't feel like accepting God's will, even though deep down I would prefer to accept it." Paul of the Cross speaks of the same struggle when he says, "I want to ready myself for whatever may happen. I resign and abandon myself to God's good pleasure. If he wants my work done, fine. If he wants it undone, let it be as he wills it. But I am in great distress and need prayers" (II, 290). Paul was accepting God's will, but he did not feel this acceptance. All he felt was distress. Yet he could make the necessary distinction between his will of free choice and his feelings, or natural preferences, and be at peace deep within himself, even with feelings of distress on the surface. We need to learn how to find that same peace when our feelings make it rough for us and when it is hard to believe we are accepting God's will.

When Paul speaks of rejoicing in God's will, he makes this same distinction between will and feelings. He refers to them as the upper and lower part of our spirit. He writes to Rose of Gaeta, "The faithful soul rejoices in the upper part of the spirit to be crucified with Christ. But do not be worried by the resistance from the inferior part of the spirit. Resist the evil suggestions of the enemy with a pure act of your will without, however, trying to force your head or your interior. In the time of these trials, it is the best thing to cast our will into the loving bosom of divine goodness" (I, 392).

Our will is the switch given us by God to control and regulate our feelings, but unfortunately the sin in which we were all born has disrupted this process. Our natural tendency is to let our feelings control our will. For example, we tend to form our plans each day according to our natural desires, which are ruled by our feelings, as we said before. We do not pause before making plans to consider what God might prefer and then by our will of free choice, surrender all our plans to him, whether our feelings like this arrangement or not. Here is a big source of inner conflict in all of us. Paul tries to forestall that conflict in the letter quoted above by the advice he gives that woman.

Feelings Change Slowly

It is important to understand clearly this distinction between our will and our feelings; our will which is free, and our feelings, which are not so free. This is so that we may not get discouraged when we find that we are really to choose something unpleasant God is asking of us, and yet find our feelings kicking up a storm of protest. We need to be patient with the gradual process by which our feelings surrender to our will.

This process might be compared to what goes on when the coil on an electric stove is red hot after we have cooked something on it, and we want to bring it to room temperature so that no one will get burned by touching it. To do this, we simply turn the switch off. Our will is like the switch. It controls our actions. Our feelings are like the coils. When we turn the switch of our will on, the coils of our feelings get hot, but it takes a bit of time. Likewise when we turn the switch off, our feelings cool down, but this takes time also, perhaps much time. This is especially true if our will and feelings had been going in one direction for many years and we decide to change that direction. The will can change quickly by the grace of God, but the feelings take much more time, perhaps months or even years.

Suppose, for example, that we had never chosen to have our plans changed by interruptions or by whatever cause. We might have tolerated such situations if we had to, but never fully chosen them. But now, by the grace of God, we have come to see these interruptions as God's will for us at the moment. We turn the switch of our will and choose such interruptions for the future. But it still takes time before our feelings go along, perhaps much time, if they have been set in that direction for many years or even a lifetime. Here is where we need patience with ourselves and an awareness that God does not expect our feelings to change quickly.

Here is another example. Perhaps we had never accepted the cross of having a phone ring when we are busy. We may have just presumed that things like this should not happen, since we have been programmed to think that way (or perhaps not to think and just presume), and we see that just about everyone else seems to think that way too. But somewhere along the line God gives us the light to see that he is the one behind the phone call and we need to learn to accept such interruptions willingly. By his grace, we then can change our attitude. We turn the switch off. Now we are willing to accept such phone calls and the coils on the stove begin to cool off. But the whole process takes time. Our feelings have been going in the opposite direction for years and they do not quiet down overnight. When we hear the phone ring at a busy time, we may catch ourselves tensing up and saying, "Oh no, not again." But that is our feelings talking. They have not completely cooled down. They will in time, since we have the switch off, but we need patience. Here is where we can get discouraged if we think that God is displeased with us if we don't change our feelings and actions immediately. But he is not displeased. He knows far better than we that the process takes much time. Once we know that this is what is going on and that God understands and expects it, we will have much more peace and patience with ourselves.

God's Will is our Guide, not Feelings

We have many kinds of feelings that give us trouble. Fears and anxieties we usually notice right away, especially if they are strong. But we also have many desires and preferences which are not according to God's will. Since these are not as strong as our fears, we often don't notice that they are even there. But they too have to be put in line with God's will by the power of the Holy Spirit. Paul speaks of them in this way to a married woman he was directing: "Do your best to rid yourself of every desire save that of pleasing God. Eat, drink and sleep as your needs require, to give pleasure to God. Abandon yourself entirely to his most holy will, leaving all cares to him. But do with diligence the work each day requires" (I, 44).

Our natural tendency is to form our plans each day according to our own natural desires, which are ruled by our feelings. We do not pause before making plans to consider what God might prefer and then surrender all our plans to him. Here is a big source of inner conflict. Paul tries to forestall this conflict by his advice to that woman.

On another occasion, Paul refers to our inner conflict with desires in this way, "The greatest perfection of a soul consists in a true abandonment of one's whole self into the hands of the Supreme Good. This abandonment includes a perfect resignation to the divine will in all the events which happen. If some desire stirs in your heart and arouses an anxiety to do something that is not in your power for the moment, let it die in the holy will of God" (I, 49).

For example, suppose we are stuck in a line of bumper-to-bumper traffic. We cannot actually do anything to change the situation. (Blowing the horn might relieve the tension a bit, but it is bound to annoy others.) In this situation it is our inner attitude which makes all the difference in the world. We can churn away inside without a thought that God has anything to do with this, and presume that things just should not be this way, or we can see the whole circumstance as God's loving will and accept the time it takes for the traffic to work itself out. So much depends on whether we have really abandoned ourselves to God's will in all things and are aware that it is God's will that we wait under these circumstances. We let our own desires get ahead of us instead of surrendering all our desires to God and trusting him for the outcome.

Paul of the Cross was much influenced in this particular area by St. John of the Cross, who devotes chapter after chapter in his Ascent of Mount Cannel, which Paul knew well, to the damage done in us by desires which are not totally subordinated to God's will. Throughout our lives we have had so many such desires and they seem so natural to us that we just take them for granted as normal — like the desire to avoid getting caught in a traffic jam. We say in the Our Father, "Thy will be done." And we know that it is his will that we carry our cross each day after Jesus. But it has probably never dawned on us that being caught in a traffic jam is precisely one of the crosses that the Lord is asking us to accept. He has a purpose behind it that we cannot see. It certainly is much easier than crucifixion. If we wait till someone scourges us, puts a beam on our shoulders, hammers nails into our hands, and so forth, we will doubtless wait forever. We need to remember that the cross comes in a modern guise (or perhaps disguise) for each of us.

Let us take another example, which we can perhaps connect more easily with Jesus' experience in his Passion. We all naturally desire that people should be nice to us. But even this desire needs to be subordinated to God's will. If we are following in the footsteps of Jesus, we will have some who are nice to us, but there will be others who will not like or treat us well at all. During his Passion Jesus had those who loved him dearly, especially the women who stood at the foot of the cross. But he also had those who hated the ground he walked on. He saw it as His Father's will that he have both kinds, so we must need both kinds too. We need to leave it up to God, as Jesus did, which persons will act in each of these ways towards us, with many shades and degrees in between. When we notice a repugnance for the way some people treat us (repugnances and aversions are really desires in reverse), then we need to submit that repugnance to the healing power of the Spirit.

Acceptance is in the Will, not the Feelings

We have to keep in mind, though, something Paul spoke of previously, and that is that our acceptance of God's will is primarily in the upper part of our spirit, our will, and not in our feelings. They take a long time to heal and to become completely subordinated to the loving will of God. They are programmed to put ourselves and our own comfort and convenience first, and not God's loving plans, especially when those plans do not look like love to our limited vision.

Even good desires, or desires for something good, have to be put in line with God's will. We often presume that because a certain desire is for something good, it must be from the Lord. But this is not always the case. Something may be good, but God may want some other good from us. Paul speaks of this aspect of our desires to Thomas Fossi, "You are full of holy desires and good intentions. Great! But we must let all of these die in the divine will. Leave them in a corner of your heart. If God wants them, he will show you, even by great wonders if necessary. But the important thing is to be ready at all times for what he wants of you" (I, 645).

Sometimes letting go of a good desire is the very thing God asks of us in order to purify us of our tendency to seek self instead of him. He may want, as Paul says, to fulfill that desire at a later time, or perhaps — and this is harder for us — to fulfill it through someone else so that they get the credit and we don't. Our desires should be that God's works are accomplished, whether now or later on according to his timetable, and by anyone God chooses, not necessarily ourselves.

We have many good desires and cannot fulfill all of them. Just because they are good does not mean that they do not have a certain amount of self-seeking mixed in with them. Paul's remedy for this was to bury all desires in God's will. The desire for God's will was for him the one absolute. All other desires were conditioned on that one. He writes again to Thomas Fossi, "All holy desires can be reduced to only one: to do in all things the most holy will of God. Burn all other desires in this holy fire and continue clothed with the sufferings of Jesus, our Savior" (I, 608).

It is not without reason that Paul here makes a connection between burning our desires in the fire of God's will and being clothed with the sufferings of Jesus. To have unfulfilled desires is certainly a suffering. This is one of the many unbloody sufferings which form part of our Passion as we follow Jesus. It was in the Passion of Jesus, which he contemplated daily, that Paul drew his lights on all these secrets of the interior life.

We Need God's Help

Though he was constantly urging those he directed to do God's will in all things, he also kept reminding them that this was something they could not do by their own unaided strength. Paul never saw the interior life as a "do-it-yourself" project or as a "go-it-alone" journey. In order to do God's will, we must be aided and led by him in everything. He is the one who enables us to do what we cannot do of ourselves. As the prophet Isaiah puts it, "O Lord, it is you who have accomplished all we have done" (26:12). When we seek his will, this will is not only light to guide us, but food to nourish and strengthen us. We have seen how much Paul loved the words of Jesus in this regard and how often he quotes them, "My food is to do the will of him who sent me" (Jn 4:34).

Paul writes this directive to Sister Cherubina Bresciani, "The way to enrich yourself with graces in the midst of interior and exterior sufferings is to nourish yourself on the divine will, even when it places you on the cross with your beloved Jesus. He himself could say, "My food is to do the will of him who sent me"(I, 491).

Another comparison Paul draws from food to help understand the effects of God's will on us is the comparison between the relish we usually have for food and the taste the Holy Spirit gradually gives for the will of God. "The food of eternal life is doing the will of God. God seasons it with various spices, savory to the spirit, though bitter to self-love. They are the trials he sends to his more beloved souls to bring them to their full perfection" (I, 491).

Joy in Suffering

The whole experience of joy in God's will, especially joy in suffering is a mysterious one, which is doubtless fully understood only by those who actually do experience it. The saints and the Scriptures often speak of rejoicing in sufferings. This can be discouraging to those who don't find any joy in suffering and presume they are just not holy. However it is good to remember that the saints, Paul of the Cross included, call it a joy in the upper part of the spirit. It is not something that can be cultivated or whipped up, but is a gift of the Holy Spirit. Paul would have us accept God's will as totally as we can and not look for any joy. Whatever joy of spirit the Lord wants us to have will come in time.

Far from rejoicing in our sufferings, most of us tend to be afraid that they will be too much. Paul was sure that this would never happen, but that God would always give us the strength to bear whatever trials he would send. Sacred Scripture too reminds us of this, "God is faithful and will not let you be tried beyond your strength; but with the trial he will also provide a way out, so that you may be able to bear it" (1 Cor 10:13). Paul emphasizes this truth to Mrs. Girolama Ercolani whom he directed for many years. "We need great acceptance of the most holy will of God in all our troubles. He arranges things for our greater good and he also knows how to give us his own consolation when we are least expecting it" (II, 589). As our love of God grows and especially our awareness of his love for us, fear of anything that his will might ask of us is bound to decrease. If he loves us, he could never let anything be too much for us. His will is all love.

Discerning God's Will

God's will is found not only in situations and events which are beyond our control, but also in situations that are under our control. Here is where we need to know how actively to do God's will. God did not make us to be robots with no freedom. We can love only to the extent that we are free. We desire to love God and to please him, but we need to know as far as possible what does please him in each circumstance. When we know it, then we can respond to it with creative initiative and full use of the freedom he has given us.

God enables us to use our freedom to direct the course of many situations. But to use our freedom in order to act lovingly, we must know what the loving thing is, what God's preference is, since what he wants is always love. The process by which we seek to know God's will is called discernment. God shows his will and his preferences only to those who really want to know his desires and plans. Paul speaks of this too. "In important matters especially, we must seek clear lights from God. It happens often that we do not do the will of God, but our own, since we don't seek to know God's will by much prayer, seeking counsel, and much reflection" (II, 374).

One question that naturally comes to our minds here and which came often to the minds of those Paul directed was this: "How do we know we are doing God's will? What is the sign?"

Peace: The Sign of Acceptance

For Paul, the big sign was peace. When seeking to know what Paul has to say about the sign that we are accepting God's will, it is important to remember that he is speaking to those who have already surrendered themselves to God in faith and desire to know and do

God's will. For others, peace would not be a sign of accepting God's will, but a sign that they were getting the things their own will desired at the moment. These people may have a temporary peace in their own pleasures and in external circumstances being smooth, but no true and lasting peace. For those whose primary goal is to love God, though, peace in the heart, even under trying circumstances, is a sign of acceptance of God's holy will. Since the ones Paul was directing were in this category, he spoke of peace as their sign. When the heart is at peace, then we are heading in the right direction. When it is not, we need to keep on looking. Paul explains this: "When you notice that your heart is moving away even the tiniest bit from that inner peace that comes from the living faith-experience of the divine presence in the soul, stop and examine what the cause of this anxiety might be. Maybe it is some worry concerning your house or children, or some situation you cannot change at the moment. Bury it in God's loving will" (I, 49).

Paul speaks of peace in the heart. It is good to note here that Paul does not speak of the heart as a symbol for the feelings, as is often done today. For Paul, the heart is deeper than the feelings. It is a symbol of our power of choice where our freedom lies, the very power by which we choose to love, whether our feelings go along or not. Feelings are very changeable and can come and go with the slightest breeze. But what is in the heart stays there permanently unless we choose to change it. For this reason there can be peace in the heart even if there is disturbance in the feelings. The heart is like the depths of the ocean where there is always calm, even though the waters on the surface may be troubled by violent storms.

Jesus in Gethsemane is the prime example of this. Before leaving the upper room, Jesus spoke of leaving his disciples his peace, not an external peace such as the world can give in pleasant situations, but a deep inner peace in the will even under the most painful situations. He himself was about to enter the most painful situation of his life, and yet he could say to his disciples, "Peace I leave with you, my peace I give to you. Not as the world gives do I give it to you. Do not let your hearts he troubled or afraid" Jn 14:27).

Yet Jesus' own feelings were very troubled and afraid. John's Gospel speaks of this in the brief struggle he shows Jesus having with the Father's will (12:27). The other evangelists present it even more vividly in their accounts of Gethsemane. Jesus' feelings were upset, terribly upset, but his heart, the deepest core of his being, was at peace. The sign for Paul of the Cross that we are on God's wavelength is peace in the heart such as Jesus had, not necessarily peace in our feelings.

Peace in God's Silence

Peace as a sign is not always easy to understand. Most of us would like some clear external sign, or even, perhaps, some sign in our feelings. We are much more aware of our feelings than we are of the depths of our heart, so a sign deep in our heart is not too reassuring. This is especially true when our feelings seem to be telling us the opposite to that sign, or when perhaps are no feelings at all to speak of. We have to accustom ourselves to the absence of feeling — at least of reassuring feelings — and become aware that we have peace deep down in our hearts. When we want to please God and do his will, then the very absence of feeling is a sign that we are moving in the right direction. If we were not, he would let us know, not by uncertain feelings, but by a full awareness that we were deliberately and purposefully rejecting his will, or at least refusing to be open to the possibility that some course of action might be his will. God's silence is the chief sign he gives us that we are on the right road.

It is somewhat like the sign our bodies give us that we are in good physical health. Ordinarily if we are in good health we feel nothing — no pain, no fatigue, no dizziness, no pins and needles anywhere. When there is nothing unusual present, we presume our health is good and ordinarily it is. We can easily accept this type of sign in discerning our bodily condition, but it is so hard to accept a similar type of sign where our spiritual condition is concerned.

When we are inwardly at peace, it seems to us that God is silent. The silence of God is really a good sign; it is a sign of inner peace. But we often become uncomfortable when God is silent, especially if in the past, God has given us glowing feelings as a sign of his presence. It is something like Peter on the Mount of Transfiguration feeling so great that he wanted to camp there and build three shacks to hang onto his delightful inner experience. But when the cloud (which to the Jews was a symbol of God's presence ever since the days of the Exodus) came over them, Peter realized that the great feelings he had had were only temporary and he became afraid. We are all like this in similar situations after we have some great feeling of God's presence and then it goes.

Growing Away from Feelings

Most of us experience wonderful things in our feelings in the early part of our journey to God. But God has to take away these feelings in the purifying process so that we will learn to walk by faith, which is a sure and certain guide, and not by feeling, which can be so deceptive. Here the human tendency is to strive might and main to recapture those feelings as a sign that we are on the right road. But they are not the sign. God's silence is. Once we are well on the way along our inner journey, God says nothing if we are on the right road. He gives signs only if we are beginning to stray off the course.

It is something like the signs they often put at the end of exit ramps on freeways, which say in big red letters, WRONG WAY. But did you ever see a sign which said RIGHT WAY? We don't need a sign if we are on the right way. It is the same on our journey along the way which is Jesus. If we were on the wrong road, God would let us know — clearly and certainly — not in "maybe's" or "perhaps he is speaking and I am not hearing him," but in an inner awareness in which we would know for certain that we were refusing to listen to him. If that awareness is not there, then we are on the right road.

One reason we tend to look for signs and fail to notice God's inner silence as a sign is that much past teaching in the Church has presumed that not only are our feelings programmed wrong, but also our conscience. It has been presumed that if we do what our conscience tells us without some reassurance from some other source, especially authority, we can deceive ourselves and are probably on the wrong road. While it is true that our feelings have been programmed to selfishness and not to God's love, yet once our inner spirit has surrendered to the Lord, then the Holy Spirit is active within us. If we listen to him within, then we have changed our programming and can safely follow what our inner spirit and conscience are telling us. Then, when God is silent, we will be secure in continuing on the path we had been following.

Jesus cried out on the cross, expressing his agonized feelings in the words, "God, my God, why have you forsaken me?" (Mt 27:46). The Father answered him by being silent. Jesus heard that silence as the Father's reassurance that he was on the right way and continued on the same course till he gave up his last breath.

But suppose we are not on the right way. What signs does God give to let us know this? We have already seen at the beginning of this chapter that Paul wants us to notice even the tiniest disturbance within us: the slightest anxiety or lack of peace, and then to stop and examine what is the problem. If the anxiety is only in our feelings and not in our will, there is no problem, since feelings of themselves are not a sign, as we have said before. But sometimes feelings can give us a clue that our will, our choice for something God is asking, or maybe asking of us, has not yet been made. For example, suppose we are going to have to explain something before a little gathering of friends in a home and we are nervous about it. The nervousness in our feelings can be a clue for us to examine what is in our will, our attitude of free choice. This examining cannot always be done on the spot, but perhaps afterwards as we look back on the situation. If we see that we were really nervous because we thought that perhaps others might think we were stupid, then we need to look to see if we had chosen the possibility of others thinking less of our intelligence .Jesus was considered a fool too, and we need to ask if we had accepted fully that possibility for ourselves. If we had, then the feelings are no sign at all. But if we had not, then the feelings are a clue to the sign in our inner attitude of choice that needs to be changed to correspond to Christ's attitude towards similar situations.

We need to notice these little signs of lack of peace. They are signs that we have not yet given the situation totally to the Lord. Once we notice them and give him our willingness for the "whatever" of the situation, then we will gradually come to peace.

But suppose it is a bigger situation and we are concerned about what to do for the future. Should we keep on what we are doing or should we change? Paul addresses this aspect of the problem too. "When a soul tries its best to be united to God and on the other hand finds no peace in the tasks and in the place where it is, it is a sign that his divine majesty desires something else of it" (Bolletino 9, 1928, 40). God will make sure we know when he wants us to change the direction in which we are heading. He will do this just as surely as do the big signs on the highway that tell us there is a detour ahead, or to warn us of construction.

Trusting God's Silence

We need to learn to live in the silence of God, trusting that all is well between him and ourselves and not searching for special signs. He loves us and will not let us be deceived or deceive ourselves as long as we are listening and really want to do his will.

God acts like a mother with a little child playing on the floor. Suppose the child notices a box which intrigues him. As he reaches for the box, he looks at his mother to see how she will react to his initiative. If he sees her looking at him and saying nothing, he keeps on reaching and takes the box to explore it. But if the box has something valuable or dangerous in it, the mother will certainly let the child know, even by strong measures if necessary, that he is not to touch the box.

God does the same with us. He never takes his loving eye off us and he knows immediately when we are in the slightest danger. If he is saying nothing, then we can continue along the course we are following. If we are doing something, we can go ahead. If we are doing nothing, we can continue this too. He will let us know when to go, to stop or to change direction. His Holy Spirit guides us at all times.

However, this comparison presumes that the child looks at his mother to find out if what he is doing is all right. We need to keep looking at God in prayer to be sure we are catching his messages. It is in peaceful prayer that we hear the Lord. Paul writes in this vein, "When you have lights in prayer that some course of action you have been following is no longer the will of God, then discern carefully. If these lights come when your spirit is calm, then follow them" (I, 223).

Wait for Calmness

A good rule to follow when we are upset is to do nothing until we are calm, even if we have to wait a day or two. Then look back at the situation at which we were disturbed and ask the Lord for light to see the situation as he sees it. When we decide what to do or not do about it and there is peace in our heart (though not always in our feelings), then that decision is from the Lord. He never hides his will from those who look for it.

Another good rule is this: If we are doing something such as desk work, cooking, cleaning, working at a machine, or whatever, and we notice that we are uptight, it is a good idea to stop just briefly and ask ourselves why. It could be that we are trying to do in fifteen minutes what God is asking us to do in a half hour or more. We need to accept God's will for whatever time our work at the moment takes. But the flip side of the coin is to let go of the possibility of doing what we would have preferred to do (or not do) with the rest of the time. This letting go is God's will too.

Desire for God's Will

The more we seek God's will, the more our desire for it will grow. Paul speaks of his own desire in a letter to Agnes Grazi. "Oh, my child, if you only knew how much I want to do God's holy will in all things! All my poor prayers are directed to no other end. I seek nothing else. I long for nothing else save in all things to be transformed by love in the divine will. I pray that my daily bread may be to do his beloved and adorable will and to do it with the greatest perfection" (I, 148). Paul did his best to inculcate this longing for God's will into every heart he directed.

The ultimate goal, as Paul saw it, was to be totally one with God's will, married to God's will as he puts it. "Take the most sweet and most holy will of God as your spouse. Be wedded to it at every moment with the ring of faith, in which are embedded the other jewels of hope and love" (I, 591).

The comparison with marriage was not merely an academic one for Paul. It was one he experienced deep down. He could grow rapturous when speaking of God's will. He loved to express himself to his God, and to pour forth his desire to please him: "O sweet will, O most gentle will, I love you, I adore you! I will what you will" (I, 392).

Paul did not expect everyone he directed to have the same depth of love for God's will as he had. But he did expect that if they were to make any progress on the journey of faith, that they would take God's will, not their own feelings, as their goal.

CHAPTER 6

The Passion in Our Lives

We might expect someone with the title "of the Cross" after his name to pay special attention to the Passion and to its chief symbol, the cross. Paul certainly does, not only by focusing on the cross of Jesus, but on the crosses in our own lives. In his spiritual direction he emphasized primarily the surrender in faith necessary to have the Spirit guide us. But he knew that the crosses that come each day are the hardest things to which we have to surrender and often the most puzzling and confusing. So he gives much attention to the crosses that are so much a part of our purification and growth.

Paul found his own light in this matter in the cross of Jesus. From that cross he heard primarily the message of God's love. God loved him and he knew it. He did his best to get that message of love across to those he directed. In the light of that love, he showed them how he saw God acting in their lives. He never saw unpleasant events in life as something that merely happen. Nor does he connect them primarily with the human beings through whom trials often come. For Paul, they are connected primarily with God. He saw them as a necessary part of our purification and growth.

He saw these trials too as an invitation to share in the Passion of Jesus, in the way they are described in the First Letter of Peter (4:12-13): "Beloved, don't be surprised at the fiery ordeal which has come among you to test you, as if something strange were happening; instead, rejoice in so far as you're sharing in Christ's sufferings, so that when his glory is revealed you may rejoice and exult." Paul of the Cross wrote in a similar vein to Agnes Grazi, "How good it is to remain on the cross with Jesus" (I, 139). Acceptance of the trials of life as our crosses to carry after Jesus was a basic part of Paul's spiritual direction.

Paul's own secret of being able to bear his crosses was to accept them directly from God and not from others, as we saw in Chapter 2. This is certainly not the approach most people have today, even most Christians. It is only natural for us to look at the human source of our sufferings: other people who are afflicting us in some way, unpleasant weather, circumstances which frustrate our plans, sickness, interior darkness and desolation, the disappointments of life, and so on. Paul always counseled not to look at the agents of our suffering that were visible to us, but at God who stands invisibly behind each one.

Paul wrote to Thomas Fossi, "Don't take your trials from creatures, but take them directly from the hand of God. He uses creatures as his instruments. Love the divine will in the midst of naked suffering" (I, 620). Paul could do this because he saw God's love behind each trial he sent. As Paul put it to Thomas, "Adore the most holy will of God in every happening. The love of God is as strong as death {Sg 8:6]. The loving soul holds its heart turned towards heaven. Look at your trials with the eye of faith, not as coming from creatures, but from the loving hand of God" (I, 684). And, again, more specifically, "Take all the trials you suffer, whether in body or in spirit, also any storm which arises from men or devils, and all the desolation, abandonment, darkness, temptation, and so on — take them all, I say, without any intermediary, from the most gentle heart of Jesus" (I, 620).

To see sufferings as coming from God's love is a cardinal point of Paul's direction, but it is most repugnant to our human sensibilities and reason. The question naturally arises, "If God loves us, how can he want us to suffer?" Our human inclination is to presume that God does not want these things to happen. He wants us to have joy, not sorrow; pleasure, not pain; healing, not sickness.

Crosses are Necessary

Paul did not see it this way. He saw trials as necessary for us and sent by a loving God for our purification and growth. He never went into the academic problem of how evil could exist in the world with a loving God in control of all things. If he were asked how bad things could happen to good people, he would reply that things were not really bad if God brought them to good, just as he brought the Passion of Jesus to Resurrection. Nothing that has ever happened in human history could qualify as a "bad thing" more than the murder of God's own innocent Son. Yet God brought that to good. In the same way, he will bring all other seemingly "bad things" to good too.

Paul did not see the things that happened to him as "bad things" even though at times they might come from human thoughtlessness, carelessness or even malice. Paul always saw these things as God's purifying trials needed to bring about some healing or growth within us. He certainly would have agreed with the succinct way in which the English mystic, Julian of Norwich put it, even though he was not aware of her writings, "Sin must needs be, but all will be well" (Revelations, Ch. 27). He would also have liked the way in which St. Thérése of the Infant Jesus, the Little Flower, was to put it in the century after Paul, "Our sufferings do not make God happy. But he knows that suffering is necessary for us. So he allows it, while, as it were, turning away his face" (L'Esprit de Ste. Thérêse, Carmel of Lisieux, pp. 103-104).

Crosses are From God's Love

These saints, in speaking of suffering as coming from God, are only echoing the whole spiritual and mystical tradition of the Church, and what Jesus himself expressed in the Garden at the beginning of his Passion. He said to Peter, as Peter was wielding his sword against the soldiers who had come to take Jesus, "Put your sword into its scabbard. Am I not to drink the cup the Father has given me?" (Jn 18:11).

It is significant that Jesus did not say, "Am I not to drink the cup that these soldiers are giving me?" or "the cup that Annas or Caiphas or Pilate is giving me?" Jesus saw everything as coming from the hand of his Father and did not take the cup from those whom Paul of the Cross calls "intermediaries." Jesus took it directly from the hand of his Father.

Jesus knew those hands were loving hands, even though what they were offering at the moment did not look like love. He had declared to his disciples very clearly, "The Father loves the Son and has given all things into his hand" (Jn 3:35). And at the Last Supper he spoke of his own love for his disciples in terms of the Father's love for him: "Just as the Father has loved me, I, too, have loved you" (Jn 15:9). He had spoken of laying down his life for his sheep at the command of his Father (Jn 10:18), and saw nothing incompatible between the Father's love and the Father's handing him, as it were, the cross. We can hardly conceive of Jesus as saying, "Father, how can you love me if you are doing this? It must be that you really don't want this 'bad thing' to happen, but are powerless to stop it. It must be that sinful men have more power than you." Such a reaction on the part of Jesus would be unthinkable. Paul of the Cross had the same attitude as Jesus and wanted all those he directed to see and accept their crosses in the same way.

Paul wrote to his own mother about this acceptance: "I hear that you are experiencing the merciful trials of God. We have to bow our heads and kiss that loving hand which gently lightens the blow. In this union with the divine will, we dispose ourselves to receive unspeakable treasures both now and in eternity" (I, 91).

Paul counsels gratitude for the trials God sends in a letter he wrote to Agnes, "I thank the Supreme Good for the trials which his divine Majesty sends me and you. If God's will is done, all will be well" (I, 177). This last expression sounds very much like Julian of Norwich, though, as we have said, Paul had never read her writings, since probably at his time they had not yet been translated from English into Italian.

Particular Crosses

Since Paul was a practical man, he applies what he has said about acceptance of the cross to specific situations. He speaks to Thomas Fossi about financial setbacks. "I rejoice to see your beautiful resignation in the merciful visits of the Lord during your recent financial setbacks. Let us adore the divine dispensations and fortify ourselves always more with patience and resignation" (I, 627).

It is not likely that many today would see financial setbacks as purifying trials purposely arranged by God's love. Most would probably see them as bad things happening to good people and caused by a poor economic climate, poor management of funds, human carelessness or some other cause with which God had nothing to do. It changes the whole picture when we see God's loving hand behind everything. Even the stock market and the Dow Jones averages are under God's total control.

Paul speaks of domestic troubles in the same way. "Be at peace in trials within the house, in the events that happen, in accidents, in having too many mouths to feed, and so forth. Remain willingly on the cross with Jesus. The greatest trials are reserved for the greatest servants of God" (I, 528-9). Here, too, God's hand and God's love are seen in everything, but this is possible only with the eye of faith. Paul never tried to guess the particular object God had in mind in sending some particular trial, but he accepted it from God's love as purposeful and that was enough.

Paul speaks of poverty, which is doubtless easy to recognize as a cross, but it often entails something else which is not so easily recognizable. Poverty often entails helplessness in one way or other. In writing to his brother Joseph, Paul refers to Joseph's poverty and to his own helplessness, both of which he sees as crosses. "I know that you are burdened with great poverty and that poverty accepted is most pleasing to God. However, I do suffer from not being able to help you in your distress. But God wills it this way and I have to accept the will of God and be at peace in it" (II, 553).

Active Acceptance

From these words, we can see that Paul did not believe in simply remaining passive under all suffering, whether our own or the sufferings of others. The only time he remained passive was when there was nothing he could do about it. If there was any way to relieve any suffering, he believed in doing it. He even gave food away to the poor when he did not have enough for himself. Jesus tells us we must carry our cross each day, but he also invited us to come to him for help when it feels too heavy: "Come to me all you grown weary and heavily burdened, and I will refresh you" (Mt 11:28). Paul would do the same. He would have relieved the poverty of his family if he could have. The paradoxical thing about suffering is that we need to accept it from the Lord when it comes, and yet do our best to relieve it, both for ourselves and for others. God will always see to it that we have both enough suffering and enough relief.

Acceptance of trials has many degrees, as we considered when speaking of Paul's attitude towards God's will at the end of Chapter 4. Paul was never satisfied either with himself or with those he directed if acceptance of the cross was no more than bare resignation to it: "putting up with" the cross. He wanted those who followed his direction to embrace the crosses God sends with love. He writes to Thomas Fossi, "Look at every painful event in your life with the eye of living faith in the eternal good pleasure of God. Receive it with joy, caress it in spirit and unite yourself to the will of God. Even espouse this most gentle and adorable will of God with faith and holy love" (I, 627).

Once we have come to believe that we need crosses to follow Jesus every day as he himself has told us (Lk 9:23), and that all our trials and troubles come from the Father, even though human beings and inanimate creatures may be his instruments, then what do we do about it? For Paul, all we need is that attitude of complete acceptance. We don't even have to notice that a cross is there. There are always plenty, as he wrote to Agnes, "Believe me, daughter, crosses will never be lacking. The more you progress in the service of God, the more suffering will increase. This was the life of Christ and this is the life of the servants of the Lord. Embrace, therefore, with good heart, the holy cross" (I,110-1).

Once there is total acceptance of any one particular cross, then even if it should come, it can no longer make us unhappy. It is our acceptance that opens our hearts wider and wider to the power and grace of the Holy Spirit to be able to bear any particular cross and even to love it. Even the disappointments of life change with acceptance. When we accept something in advance, like the non-arrival of a letter we are expecting, for example, and are ready for it by the grace of the Spirit, it is no longer disappointing if the letter doesn't come. However, total surrender is a long process, and for some kinds of crosses, even a lifelong process.

Joy and Peace in Suffering

It might seem from Paul's statement to Agnes about the increase in sufferings that Paul expected life to become more and more unhappy for anyone who wanted to follow Christ more closely. But it was just the opposite. Paul writes, "How great our joy when we make a little progress walking the royal road of the cross!" (I, 172). Paul himself was a cheerful person and, like St. Teresa of Avila whom he admired so much, he had no use for "sour-faced saints."

How do we know that we are on that road and that we are really accepting the crosses God is sending, especially if we don't feel like accepting them at all, and perhaps say, "I don't want them," meaning, "I have no natural preference for these crosses at all"? When we catch ourselves saying these things, it is easy to put ourselves on a guilt trip as if God must be displeased with us. But he knows we cannot help our feelings. The sign we are on the right road is not feeling good about any particular cross, hut — as we considered in the last chapter on God's will — the sign is peace deep within the heart.

However, this peace is not something we get completely and all of a sudden, but something that usually comes by degrees. It is something like the way the ocean calms down after a storm. The waves are tremendous during the storm, but once the winds start to die down, the waves begin to lessen. If the storm has been really violent, the waves may still be above normal for even a few days afterwards. We can do something, though, that the ocean cannot. We can accelerate the process. How do we do this?

We first need to become comfortable when our own feelings (and our heart deep down) are at peace, knowing that we are accepting whatever God may be asking of us at the moment. Then when a storm comes, great or small, we need to expect it and not become discouraged because a new storm has arisen. The storm is not a sign that we are getting worse, or going backwards on our journey towards God, but that some situation has surfaced an attitude inside us that was there all along, but not noticed. God saw it, though, and is now bringing about the circumstances to make it surface so that we can see it and give it to him to change. It is good if we can remain at peace. However, if we are emotionally upset, it may be hard to notice any peace we might have deep down. Therefore it is good to wait till we are comparatively calm and then reflect to see exactly what it was that upset us.

When we take a closer and calmer look at the situation, we can usually see that it was a cross that we had never fully accepted as part of our life. For example, it might be that we are upset over some derogatory remark that has just been passed about us. If we are, it might mean that we had never fully chosen that aspect of the Passion before, viz., having derogatory remarks or even insults leveled at us as Jesus did. We need to take a second look at the situation, but this time in the light of faith. By the grace of God, we can usually see that we were not facing the situation with an attitude similar to that of Jesus. Also by his grace we can change our attitude to conform to that of Jesus and accept for the future what we had not previously accepted in the past.

Crosses Never too Much

We certainly do not need, according to Paul, to go looking for crosses. There are always enough. Jesus himself said this after his beautiful lesson on the birds of the air and the lilies of the field. "One day's troubles are enough for a day" (Mt 6:34). Notice the word enough. Not too many, not too few. Just enough. For some it might seem that there are not enough, but for most of us, it would probably seem that there are too many. But Paul of the Cross emphasized, as did his namesake Paul the apostle, that God never sends too many.

In saying that God never sends too many crosses or too heavy a cross, Paul was also echoing St. Francis de Sales, whom he read and loved. This great saint said that God measured every cross to the tiniest millimeter, weighed it to the tiniest milligram, looked at the strength of the one to whom he was sending it, and then sent with it the grace to bear it.

It is basic to Paul's direction that all our trials and troubles come ultimately from God's loving hands, even though other persons, possibly even sinful persons, like Judas for Jesus, maybe God's instruments. Since this is the case, Paul expects from those he directs a willingness to embrace every trial from God's love as a temporary purification for an eternal growth of love. He expects that they choose it in the upper part of their spirit, their power of free choice, even though their feelings may find the cross repugnant. For him, this was the way to great peace, purification and growth in love. The whole process was an invitation from God to share in the Passion of Jesus and to be filled with love.

CHAPTER 7

The Passion in Prayer

Paul of the Cross wanted the Christ-like attitudes of love for God's will and acceptance of the crosses of daily life to sink always more deeply into the hearts of those he directed. For this reason, he wanted them to reflect, often, long, and deeply, on the Passion of Jesus. He wanted them to do this, not as an intellectual exercise or study, but as prayer — as communication with Jesus personally in the light of the Passion. He wrote to Agnes, "I dearly desire that the object of your prayer should be the Passion of Jesus Christ in loving dialogue with him. But understand me well. I want to leave you free to follow the loving attractions of the Holy Spirit. We must pray not in our way, but in God's way" (I, 112).

The Passion is Love

For Paul, meditating on the Passion was meditating on love. It was looking at the Passion to see love there. It was, as he said to Agnes, a "loving dialogue," that is, a conversation between lovers. The Passion for Paul was never merely a past event, though certainly its outward circumstances are past. It was a present love-mystery. The outward events of the Passion were a sign then of the love of Jesus to those who had the faith to see this, and they are still such a sign to those who have faith. The events are past, but the love is present. For Paul, the Passion is *now*.

He wrote to Thomas Fossi, "Always bring with you to prayer some mystery of the most holy life and Passion of Jesus Christ. Then, if the Holy Spirit draws you to deeper recollection, follow the breath of the Holy Spirit, but always through the means of the Passion. This way you will avoid all deception" (I, 791).

What does Paul mean by the "mystery" of the Passion in writing to Thomas? A divine mystery is not like a mystery in a detective story. There we have an enigma which most people can't solve, but is finally solved by some smart detective. A divine mystery is an excess of light in which we see light and truth, but know that there is always more to be discovered — limitlessly more. It is like the mystery of the ocean, or the mystery of outer space. We are constantly making more discoveries in both of these areas. But the more we discover, the more we find that is yet to be discovered. Divine mysteries are like that. The more we see into them, the more we know, the more we also find is yet to be known. Mysteries exceed even the deepest penetration of our minds. Yet we need to continue the process of depth-penetration to discover always more of God's truth and love.

The Passion is a mystery which throws the greatest light on God's love that was ever shed by any human event, yet no matter how deeply we penetrate this mystery, there is always more to it. The Passion as a whole was one big event, but it was composed of shorter events from Gethsemane to Calvary. Each happening can manifest its own particular light as we ponder it. We need to consider it, though, not merely by thinking of it as an historical occurrence, such as the scourging, for example, but by trying to understand what went on in Jesus' heart in this event. How did he feel? What were his attitudes, his choices?

He himself gives us some idea of this in his first proclamation of his impending Passion, according to Matthew's Gospel: "From then on Jesus began to explain to his disciples that he had to go on to Jerusalem and suffer terrible things at the hand of the elders, the chief priests and scribes and be put to death and rise on the third day" (Mt 16:21). Notice the words "had to go on." Jesus accepted his Passion in its entirety as something that had to be. Even when Peter tried to persuade him that it should not be that way, he said to Peter in strong words: "Get behind me, Satan! You're not judging by God's standards but by men's" (Mk 8:33).

Jesus expressed the same attitude to the two disciples on the road to Emmaus after his resurrection. "Didn't the Messiah have to suffer all these things and enter into his glory?" (Lk 24:26). Jesus saw his Passion and all that it entailed as something necessary in God's plan and he accepted it that way in all its details. This means that he accepted the agonizing fear and depression which he experienced in Gethsemane. He accepted the loss of his freedom when they bound him. He chose to experience injustice in his trials and to have lies told about him. He chose the scourging and the ridicule of the crowning with thorns. He accepted rejection by his own people whom he loved dearly. He accepted a death in torment and disgrace which would turn many of his disciples away from him. And he would end his life a seeming failure in the eyes of all. These are just some of the many, many details of the Passion embraced by the will of Jesus. Each is part of the mystery and each can provide us with its own light and strength when we ponder it from Jesus' perspective. This is what Paul of the Cross wanted all those he directed to do.

Notice that Paul includes the life of Jesus with the Passion. He was aware that the whole life of Jesus from the manger to the grave was a sign of God's love. Any one incident in the life of Jesus could provide fruitful meditation and might be more apropos for a particular situation. When Paul wrote to people during the Advent and Christmas seasons, he certainly spoke of the mystery and message of the infancy of Jesus and urged meditation on these mysteries. But it was the Passion which was for him the greatest source of light and love. So Paul concentrated on that and recommended this same focus to those he directed.

Let the Spirit Lead

Paul presumes that those who give themselves to meditating on the Passion of Jesus and drinking in its love will be led by the Holy Spirit to deeper and deeper prayer. That is why he constantly adds to his recommendations to meditate on the Passion that there should be freedom to follow the guidance of the Holy Spirit.

For Paul prayer was not so much work as it was relaxation, that is, relaxing in the arms (or the bosom, as he would say, and as will be explained more fully in the next chapter) of someone we love. He presumed that if someone were faithful to prayer, the Holy Spirit would speak in their hearts and they would only have to relax to drink in the message of the Spirit, "in spirit and in truth," as he often put it, using the words of Jesus to the Samaritan woman at the well (cf. Jn 4:24).

However, even when the Spirit was drawing one into deeper quiet prayer, Paul did not believe that the memory of the Passion should be ignored. "It is true that the memory of the most holy Passion of Jesus Christ with the imitation of his holy virtues should never be left aside, even in the most profound recollection and the highest gift of prayer. This, rather, is the door which leads the soul to intimate union with God, to interior recollection and to the most sublime contemplation" (I, 582).

"Memory" of the Passion

When Paul speaks of the "memory" of the Passion in this context, he obviously does not refer to detailed, imaginative meditation. He seems to be referring rather to a general awareness of the Passion and a desire to imitate Christ, especially in the virtues he exhibited in the Passion. We have to remember that Paul was not used to thinking of the Passion primarily as a past historical event, but as a present love-mystery and love-message. He wanted always to imitate the openness of Jesus in his Passion to the love of the Father and all that the Father was asking of him.

For Paul, the memory of the Passion in this way was a door to prayer, that is, to a two-way conversation with Jesus. Paul always considered the chief speaker in this conversation as Jesus, not ourselves. He writes to Sister Gerolama Ercolani, "Jesus will teach you to pray. Place yourself at his feet like a poor wounded beggar and say to him with reverence and humility, 'Dear Jesus, teach me to pray.' Then draw near with faith and holy love to his most holy wounds. Dwell in all simplicity on his most holy Passion, without forcing your mind, but gently. Jesus will teach you" (II, 577).

Writing to Thomas Fossi, Paul says that not only will Jesus teach one how to pray but that he loves to share himself in this way. True lovers always enjoy sharing with each other, communicating with each other what is deep in the heart of each. They love to be alone at times just to do this. Paul expresses this tendency of lovers when he says, "Make for yourself a most beautiful retreat in the deepest part of your spirit and in this sacred desert share with the Supreme Good one on one, adoring him in spirit and in truth (Jn 4:24). His divine Majesty enjoys sharing the mysteries of his most holy Passion" (I, 612). Paul certainly sees this prayer as deeply personal, not just an intellectual or emotional exercise. It is a personal sharing with one we love, sharing what is in our heart and listening to what is in his heart.

Paul gives an explicit example of this in another of his letters: "If you are meditating on Jesus in agony in the garden, imagine yourself there alone in that garden with him. Look at him with compassion but with lively faith and love. Collect a few drops of his precious blood and ask him, 'My dear Jesus, for whom are you suffering?' Then listen to him speak to your heart" (II, 625).

Paul's approach to all this makes meditation on the Passion much more than spiritual gymnastics to develop virtues, though he does speak of virtues as the fruit of such meditation. But most of all, Paul wants those he directs to engage in warmly personal relaxed conversation with Jesus, taking it for granted that Jesus will speak to them too.

How to Start

We might ask, "Doesn't Paul give any advice or even some hints about how to begin such love conversation?" He does. Paul was not one to give many rules for meditation, but at times he does give suggestions that are quite detailed. His recommendations are warmly personal, as we can see from the following examples.

In writing to Anna Cecilia Anguillara, Paul must have been answering a problem she had with using a book for meditation. Paul was not adverse to using a book to get started, but he did not want anyone to become dependent on a book. So he writes, "Don't take it as a bad sign when you can't remember what you have read in the meditation book. Approach it in this way. After you have read the meditation and have already forgotten what you have read (something that happens even to holy souls), humble yourself as a poor little one before God and ask him for an alms. Do this mentally with a peaceful spirit. Then (for example), begin your prayer this way: 'O sweet Jesus, how did your divine heart feel in that agony in the garden? My soul! A God sweating blood for you! A God in agony for you! Oh love! Oh great Father, how much have you loved and still love my soul! And I have offended you! How ungrateful! Ah sweet Jesus, wash me with your precious blood, burn me with your holy love!'

"All these things I propose as examples, understanding that in all these outpourings of affection, you should not be in a hurry, but make them slowly, with an interior spirit, stopping in each of them in a silence of faith and love in the divine presence. If in one particular ejaculation you spend a quarter of an hour, oh how that time would have passed with fruit" (III, 214).

He gives similar directions to Mrs. Marianna Alvarez, adding, as he so often did, a little personal touch, though we need to remember that the suggestions he makes are only suggestions which he believed would be adapted to her. He keeps encouraging her to freely follow the lead of the Holy Spirit: "In the morning, before beginning your mental prayer, say an Our Father and seven Hail Mary's and seven Glory Be to the Father's, and one Apostles' Creed. Throw a nod for me to all this holy company with a Glory Be to the Father, and tell them that poor Paul is also looking for an alms.

"Do this with your hands joined and your eyes raised to heaven, and say seven times: 'O Holy Spirit, Love of the Father and the Son, inflame me completely with your love.' At about noon, that is before lunch, kneel down and say seven Glory Be to the Father's. Then with hands joined and eyes lifted to heaven, say: 'O Spirit of infinite light, of infinite tenderness, come into my heart! Come, infinite good! Come, immense love! Come, true and only God with the Father and the Son! Come, immense love to dwell in my poor penitent heart! Come, my love! Come, my tenderness, my light, my life, my comfort, my only hope, my God, my all! Come because I languish with love! Come because I can no longer suffer not loving you. Come to inflame me, even to the marrow of my bones.' Then say the Creed, and afterwards salute the most holy Virgin with a Hail Mary and ask her most holy blessing. Salute her for me with a Glory Be. Do the same in the evening before beginning your mental prayer. I beg you in all these acts to let yourself be filled with a spirit of peace and love. Make them gently, and if love compels you to be silent, be silent" (I, 532).

One thing Paul always emphasizes in prayer is to do things gently. He urges that prayer be made peacefully, easily, without forcing mind or heart. It is only natural that beginners especially, if they thought they were not succeeding well in prayer, would try harder and make greater efforts to put pictures into their minds or to force feelings. Paul would have none of this. He wanted prayer to be relaxed and gentle.

Distractions

One experience that bothers just about everyone trying to pray is distractions. Paul was very consoling in this matter. God had given him lights concerning his own distractions and he used these lights for others. He puts it in this way:

"I want to explain what happens to me in distractions. When I am distracted, my soul remains more or less in peace with God, despite the fact that it is disturbed by the thoughts that trouble me. Occasionally I say to my understanding which tries to wander here and there, 'Go where you please as long as you always go with God.' I do not know how to describe what happens to me during these distractions, that is, what kind of thoughts pass through my mind during the time of prayer except when they are obvious temptations... But the will, which is the mouth through which the holy food of divine love enters, although still secretly nourished, is hindered by the disturbance arising from these two faculties of memory and understanding which wander away into distractions....

"In my opinion, it is like an infant with its mouth at its mother's breast as it takes its milk. Although it struggles with its hands and feet, fidgets, turns its head and so forth, it continues all the time to draw nourishment because it never takes its mouth away from its mother's breast. Certainly it would do much better for itself if it stayed quiet instead of acting as I have just described; nevertheless, the milk goes down its throat because it never takes its mouth away from its mother's breast.

"So it is with the soul. The will is the mouth which never fails to imbibe the milk of holy love, although the faculties: memory and understanding, wander away from it. Certainly it gains more assistance if they remain quiet and united with it" (I, 5).

Since distractions are the greatest disturbers of peace in prayer, Paul was able to comfort those who were distracted and reassure them that they were praying in spite of the distractions and that their prayer was pleasing to God. Even in banishing distractions, though, Paul wanted only gentle efforts, without worry or anxiety. For Paul, good prayer is peaceful and worry-free deep inside, even though at times it maybe very disturbed in the feelings, as was the prayer of Jesus in Gethsemane.

Variety in Prayer

Notice in all the examples Paul gives, that he was just letting his own love and his own spirit pour out. However, he never presumed that God was casting us all into the same mold. That is why he so frequently said that he wanted those he directed to be free to follow the Holy Spirit. Every prayer and ejaculation he uses, he gives only as suggested examples, presuming that these will trigger off the initiative of the one to whom he is writing and that the Holy Spirit will move them to pray in the uniquely personal way in which he is guiding them.

It is worth noting here that Catholics, even priests and religious, are often slaves to the words of the prayers they say and are afraid to let their own personal initiative and creativity come out. Written words, even inspired written words, such as the psalms, are really the prayers of the psalmist. They were inspired, yes, but more as to their spirit than to their exact words. The psalms were not all written in the same century. We have a number of cases where a psalmist would take another psalm, written in a previous century, and adapt and change it to fit the needs of his own time. We need to have that same spirit of flexibility in adapting prayers to our own needs. Paul encouraged this spirit in those to whom he suggested ejaculations or other prayers. Paul's ejaculations were really his own prayers. But he hoped that these would stimulate others to pray in their own words according to their own needs and their own spirit. Paul believed that the Lord wants to listen to what is personal in each of us, not merely to have us repeat prayers, even beautiful ones, by someone else. We need to use the words of prayers of others at times, but if we never pray in our own personal way, something is missing. It is when there is no personal creativity that prayers, whether personal or communal, tend to become monotonous and unenjoyable.

Paul gives suggestions for meditating and for entering into prayer to those who were still new at the art of prayer and needed this form of help, such as his suggestions to Marianna. But for those who were already accustomed to contemplation and to allowing the Holy Spirit to guide their prayer, he had other recommendations. For example, he writes to Sister Colomba Gandolfi, "Present yourself for prayer plunged into your own nothingness, but clothed with Jesus Christ and with his sufferings in pure faith and nakedness of spirit. Don't rely on your imagination but let your spirit make that flight of love which your heavenly Spouse will enable it to make. He who enables you to make the flight will also give the wings to make it" (II, 496).

Let God Work

Paul's whole approach to prayer was the traditional approach of the Church's great mystics, but directly contrary to the do-it-yourself mentality so common to most today. He believed that the Lord is the author of prayer. As his great namesake, Paul the apostle put it, "We don't know how to pray as we should; instead, the Spirit himself pleads for us" (Rm 8:26). Paul of the Cross was a faithful follower of this teaching both for himself and those he directed.

Yet Paul was not a quietist. Quietism was a teaching on prayer branded as erroneous by Church authority in 1687, seven years before Paul was born. Quietism taught that a person could simply go to prayer and do nothing, and presume God would act and do everything. As we can see from his suggestions for beginners, Paul presumed that we do need to do our part in communicating with God.

On the other hand, Paul did not give outlined meditations, particular Scriptures to read, specific virtues to concentrate on, as other saints have done with great fruitfulness, especially St. Ignatius. Paul was familiar with this approach, but his own method was simpler and more direct. He was not accustomed to directing groups or giving group suggestions. His directions were unique to each one and adapted to that particular person's needs. He would listen to each one, see as best he could where that person was with the Lord, and give recommendations accordingly. He would listen very patiently to his or her problems in prayer or in their journey with the Lord. He would then help that person to listen to the Lord and handle the problem as the Spirit indicated.

For light to do all this, Paul always looked to the Passion of Jesus. This showed him more deeply each time how much he was loved. And he did his best to communicate this message to others and to have them regard the Passion the same way. Contemplating the Passion also revealed to him the virtues of Jesus, his attitudes regarding various situations and his values. Paul tried to evaluate similar situations in his own life or in the lives of those he directed to see how the Passion applied to these situations. For him, the Passion was the door to prayer and the light he needed for daily living.

CHAPTER 8

The Holy Spirit

*I*n all his guidance, Paul placed special emphasis on the role of the Holy Spirit. He wrote to Francis Appiani, "The true teacher of prayer is the Holy Spirit" (I, 397). It is rare that in his letters of guidance he does not have some mention of the Holy Spirit. One of his most frequent expressions was, "I want you to he free to follow the inspiration of the Holy Spirit."

Paul believed that the Holy Spirit, God's breath of love, was constantly at work in everyone. For those who wanted to take Jesus seriously and live a life of daily prayer-communication with him, Paul knew of no better way than to surrender to the inner impulses of the Holy Spirit. The Spirit would lead them to that form of prayer which they needed at the moment.

Letting the Spirit Guide

He writes to Mother Mary Crucified, "Above all, let yourself be guided by the Holy Spirit. Remain in your own nothingness and when you sense the divine attractions and impressions, follow the invitation God gives you, at one time remaining plunged into God in a holy silence, at another time absorbed in loving wonder at the divine perfections, at another bursting forth in praises of God, at another penetrated with love and sorrow looking at the sufferings of Jesus, and so on" (II, 289).

This "nothingness" Paul speaks of is a notion that may be unfamiliar to us, even though it is biblical. Paul the apostle tells us, "If anyone thinks he is something when he is nothing, he is deluding himself" (Gal 6:3). What he is telling us is that we are nothing apart from God, but that all we have and are is God's gift. Paul of the Cross and other mystical writers often use the same expression to describe what our attitude should be toward God. We are nothing but God is everything. However, God wants to gift the nothingness which we are with all his own riches, even with his whole being. He wants to share this with us to our full capacity to accept it. As the mystics put it, God wants to take our nothingness and fill it with his ALL. Even though we may not understand this process — and it is doubtful that Paul's readers understood everything he was saying — as long as we can accept it, God is working in us.

Paul was not adverse to the idea of having those he directed make plans ahead of time for how they should pray. But he wanted those plans to be abandoned immediately when the attraction of the Holy Spirit was felt to pray in a different way. As he wrote to Francis Appiani, "The teacher of prayer is the Holy Spirit and therefore we must pray as it pleases him. When your soul feels the attraction to remain quietly lost in God in a sacred silence of love, let it be that way, because you are now listening to God in pure and naked faith. When your soul feels the attraction to dialogue lovingly on the divine mysteries, or make requests for your own needs or those of others, then do that. The important thing is to follow the loving breath of the Holy Spirit"(I, 419).

The Spirit Works in Silence

Paul did not want the following of the Holy Spirit in prayer to be confused with striving to stimulate emotional fervor. He wrote to Sister Marianna of Jesus, "When I speak of being obedient to the Holy Spirit, I don't mean that you should try to arouse feelings of devotion. Internal obedience to the Holy Spirit consists in following his inner loving impulses in holy prayer. It is especially important not to lose sight of our own nothingness and to lift ourselves in spirit where the Holy Spirit draws us with his gentle attractions. We must remain alone in our own interior, totally plunged into the immense love of God in a sacred silence of faith and love" (II, 730).

Paul knew well that when all is quiet in prayer, it is easy to presume that nothing is happening. We like to feel God's presence. But our feelings, or emotions, cannot contact God since God is spirit. They can be stepping stones to prayer, but feelings, no matter how exhilarating, are never prayer itself. Paul had to reassure those he directed that they were praying when things were quiet and that the Holy Spirit was active, even though they felt nothing.

Paul knew that troublesome distractions could also he present, but we have already seen his beautiful comparison with the baby at its mother's breast in the last chapter. As far as Paul was concerned, the condition for engaging in prayer was very simple: want to pray and you are praying, no matter what happens. God is aware of us at every moment and if he wants us to do something, he will let us know. If he does not let us know, even though we are distracted and without any noticeable feeling, we are actually praying.

If we don't feel that we are praying, we tend to use the good old axiom, "Try harder." Paul was completely opposed to this. After telling Francis Appiani that the teacher of prayer was the Holy Spirit, Paul added, "Do not strain either your mind or heart" (I, 397). He also advised that one's physical position at prayer should be relaxed and not strained.

The Spirit Teaches Us the Passion

As we have seen, Paul wanted those he directed to take with them to prayer some thought of the Passion of Jesus. For this, too, he taught them to rely on the Holy Spirit. "Always pass through the door which is the most holy life, Passion, and death of Jesus in whatever way the Holy Spirit will teach you. Prayer should not be made in our way, but as the Holy Spirit wills" (II, 818).

While Paul always wanted those he directed to meditate in some way on the Passion, he did not believe that the Passion should always be part of their prayer in the same way. It was not only that variety was needed, as we have already seen, but also that as growth in the Lord took place, the Passion would have a different place in the life of the one praying. The Holy Spirit would teach this too. Paul explains it this way:

"The best and holiest way to pray is to think of the most holy Passion of the Lord. This is the way to reach a holy union with God. But the soul must realize that it cannot always do this in the same way that it did at the beginning. It is therefore necessary to follow the impulses of the Holy Spirit and let yourself be guided as his divine Majesty wills" (I, 43).

Paul gave more detailed suggestions about meditating on the Passion to those just beginning a life of deep prayer than to those who were more advanced. Since he knew that the Holy Spirit would work more deeply in their hearts as they went along, he always suggested that they leave themselves free to pray as the Spirit was moving them and not try to cling to any particular prayers, ejaculations, or suggestions he might have made to them earlier in their prayer life.

Paul was opposed to all rigidity in prayer, as we might have noticed from the preceding statements of his. If he were living among us today, he might recommend that we "hang loose." Just when we might feel great fervor before prayer, we might end up dry as dust. And just when we might not feel like praying at all, we might have a beautiful experience of God's presence.

The Spirit Teaches Us to Listen

To pray in depth, we need inner peace. When we surrender to the Holy Spirit in peace of heart, he leads us into deep conversation with God. Paul calls this "one on one" or "alone with the alone." It is hard for twenty-first century Catholics to believe that God will speak to them. Paul believed that this would be the common experience, and even the constant experience of each and everyone who gave themselves to a life of prayer. When we love someone, we enjoy conversing with them. And this conversation is a two-way exchange, not a monologue. It is the same with God. Paul believed that we should hear God as well as speak to him.

We should not always, or perhaps even often, expect to hear words, but in the deep peace of our hearts, we can become aware of God's loving presence, as lovers can converse with each other often without words.

Here is one of Paul's beautiful expressions in this regard: "In prayer, be obedient to the inner direction of the Holy Spirit, leaving your spirit free to fly where the gentle and loving breeze of this most divine Spirit guides it. Keep your interior well quieted, peaceful and recollected, remaining alone in the chamber of your own interior, treating one on one with your beloved Good, reposing in him, losing everything in that immense ocean of love. God will teach you" (I, 493).

Fear of Deception

In all this it is only natural to have some fears that we might be deceiving ourselves and Paul was well aware that this fear was common.

He writes to Agnes Grazi, "Keep praying in the manner in which the Holy Spirit leads you. Everyone who rests in God with confidence and true humility will not he deceived" (I, 177). Paul did not believe that anyone who was open to the Lord and surrendered to his will could ever be led astray. God loves each of us and he will not let anyone be deceived. However, it does follow that if we are not willing for what the Lord wants and are not seeking to do his will, we could easily be open to deception. But if we had that attitude, we would know it.

However, Paul had to contend at times with those who wanted to pray for what seemed to be selfish reasons. The eighteenth century was an age when people thought that visions were a sign of great sanctity and strove to see visions. This type of person often engaged in prayer to impress others with a show of holiness. In dealing with people like this, Paul followed the simple rule of Jesus, "By their fruits you will know them" (Mt 12:33).

Paul expresses it this way: "Make your prayer not in your way, but in God's way. Give way to the Holy Spirit. Let your soul fly wherever the Holy Spirit leads you. Hold as suspect, no, rather as deceptions, any lights that do not leave great humility, self-knowledge, peace and a great desire to please God. Lovers speak little. One word of love can hold the soul in deep recollection for a long while" (I, 433).

Fruits of the Spirit

Paul, the apostle, gives examples of the fruits of the Holy Spirit (Gal 5:22). The chief ones he lists are love, joy and peace. If we find that our prayer makes us more capable of loving others, even those we don't naturally like, of living a happy life, even though we are bound to have ups and downs in our feelings, and of being basically at peace, then the Lord is working in us. Paul of the Cross adds humility and a willingness to share in Christ's Passion and we could add many more fruits as we begin to experience them.

It is not that we should examine ourselves introspectively to see what fruits we are bearing. Even here, though, the Holy Spirit will help us to see enough to be reassured that we are on the right road. Fear of deception is a real fear and Jesus has told us that he does not want us to live in fear (Lk 12:7). As the awareness of God's deep love for us grows, we lose all fear that we might be deceived in our prayer.

Paul of the Cross does speak of the fruit of joy which those who pray deeply are bound to experience, though he cautions us not to cling to it. He wrote to Sister Colomba Gandolfi, "In prayer always do your part with a lively faith in the immense majesty of God, as you share with him while being aware of your own deep nothingness. As you experience the loving breeze of the Holy Spirit, which absorbs your soul in his joy, let your terrible nothingness disappear into the joy of the Lord, without looking too long at the joy, but simply at its divine object. He pours it into you so that you can love him more" (II, 509).

Paul wanted those he directed to let their prayer be a real love-gift to God, not a seeking of spiritual gratification and pleasure. He believed God would give all the gifts of love and joy we need and that the more we let them go and not cling to them, the more they would return to us in greater abundance.

The Spirit Draws Us into the Passion

Paul believed that the Holy Spirit would teach in prayer many things that could never be explained in human language. To one of his own priests who was having trouble understanding how we should make our own the sufferings of Jesus, Paul wrote, "It is necessary to be most obedient to the most gentle breath of the Holy Spirit. The point that you don't understand, how to make your own by love the most holy sufferings of dear Jesus, his divine Majesty will make you understand when he pleases" (III, 149).

Paul gives a clue of this, too, when he speaks of the way the Spirit can and may draw us when we start to meditate on the Passion. He writes to Teresa Palozzi, "Regarding the mysteries of the most holy Passion, remain reflecting on them as your heart finds more devotion and your love for God enkindles more. But when your soul experiences a relish for remaining in a sacred silence of faith and holy love, reposing in the bosom of the divine Father, go that way, even though this should last for your whole prayer time. It is the Holy Spirit who draws your soul into this prayer and we must obey the attractions of the Holy Spirit" (III, 369).

Paul's experience in his own prayer and the way he directed others was that one never knows what to expect hut that we should be ready for anything. The Holy Spirit is God's own love and love enjoys surprising the beloved. Paul believed that the Holy Spirit is always drawing us more and more into intimate love-relationship with God, a marital, spousal relationship as he often called it. It makes all the difference in the world whether one looks on God as simply a source of benefits or help, or even as a "co-pilot," or whether one experiences him as the love of your life, giving life and power to all other loves. Paul believed that there are no limits to the depths of love to which the Holy Spirit will draw us if we allow ourselves to he drawn.

There is one important thing to notice in Paul's direction, which comes not from anything he says, but from what he does not say. Paul does not speak of degrees or stages of prayer. He was very familiar with Teresa of Avila and her seven mansions, or stages of prayer life. He knew well St. John of the Cross and his division of the life of prayer into the Purgative Way, or way of beginners, the Illuminative Way, or way of proficients, and the Unitive Way, or the way of the perfect. But while Paul admired Teresa and John and often quoted them, he himself never spoke of any stages of prayer. In this, he was not disagreeing with the two Spanish mystics, but he did not want those he directed to try to figure out their own progress and where they were on the spiritual ladder, as it were. He believed in teaching them to follow the guidance of the Holy Spirit and to leave their progress in his hands.

The Spirit Leads to Great Heights

Paul was eloquent, though, when he spoke of the heights to which the Holy Spirit would lead those who were faithful to the guidance of the Spirit. He wrote to Sister Cherubina Bresciani, "Keep your soul in freedom and let it pray in the manner of the Holy Spirit. When God gives lights to know better your own ungratefulness, it is a sign that he wants you to be moved to contrition. When he leaves you in freedom to speak of his Passion, do it, but with peace and gentleness, letting love and sorrow be mixed. But when God wants that the poor butterfly, after having circled around that divine flame, should be enflamed by it and there remain enjoying that sweet light, that sweet fire of love, you must let it remain that way and not awaken it from that divine sleep. "Remain in loving attention to God, from which is born that sacred silence of love which is a speech most eloquent in the ears of your divine spouse. Contemplate the divine perfection, his infinite grandeur, his immensity, his infinite beauty, goodness, and so on. Let your soul rest in loving wonder and awe, from which is born that satisfaction that God is the infinite good that he is. In this satisfaction the soul rejoices, exults, makes festival and enjoys the riches and grandeurs of her beloved good. Oh, what a great science is this, my daughter!" (I, 461).

Today we hear much about the work of the Holy Spirit as a giver of gifts, such as tongues, prophecies, healings, and so on. These gifts he bestowed on the early Church and even to some extent through the centuries. The gift of tongues was not used in Paul's time, as far as we know. But what the gift of tongues principally expresses — namely, the exultant praise of God, Paul certainly engaged in himself and encouraged in those he directed, as we can see from the previous citation. Paul possessed the gift of healing and the gift of prophecy, but he did not speak of these in connection with his spiritual direction. In fact, he did not speak of them at all and we had to learn that he possessed them from the testimony of others. But the gifts of the Holy Spirit which Paul emphasized were those which enabled a person to enter into deep, personal love-union with God in prayer, and also those which made him receptive to the constant action of God in everyday life. We will see more of this later.

CHAPTER 9

Personal Prayer

he type of prayer that Paul of the Cross normally spoke and wrote about was what we usually call "mental prayer," that is, prayer without set words. Obviously, this is personal, private prayer, since if we are praying with others we have to use words to keep together. However, words may also be used when we are praying alone, and Paul does have something to say about this. We call this type of prayer "vocal prayer," not because it has to be said aloud, but because there are set words to it, such as the Our Father or the Hail Mary.

Vocal Prayer

Paul's longest recommendation concerning vocal prayer and suggestions as to what prayers to use, he gives to Agnes Grazi in the early days of her life of prayer. The length and details of his suggestions might surprise us, but here they are:

> "Concerning vocal prayer say the following, since you have too much to do for any more.
> Five decades of the Rosary, three Our Fathers and Hail Marys to the Most Holy Trinity, thanking
> them on the part of the Blessed Virgin Mary with the three prayers, 'I adore you,' and so on.
> A Credo to the holy apostles, an Our Father and Hail Mary with a Glory Be to the Guardian Angel.
> Another to your own patron saint.
> Three Our Fathers and Hail Marys with a Glory Be, and so on, thanking the Most Holy Trinity for the graces granted

to your most holy patrons and to the whole heavenly court. In honor of the seven sorrows, say what you are accustomed to say. In honor of the wounds of Jesus, the five customary prayers. From now until Christmas (nine days) say 40 Hail Marys.

In honor of St. Francis, an Our Father and five Glory Be's. Nine Glory Be's in honor of the nine choirs of angels. On the feasts of your holy patrons, honor them with some extra devotion as the Holy Spirit inspires you." (I, 104).

This list gives us some idea of the prayer customs of the time. At that time, there was very little spontaneity in prayer among Catholics. Protestants had more of it, but Catholics did not associate with Protestants and knew little or nothing of their prayer styles. Catholics were not used to composing their own vocal prayers or exercising any personal creativity in prayer. Paul himself, though, was very spontaneous and creative, as we have seen. While not specifically mentioning spontaneity and creativity with those he directed, Paul was constantly urging them to let the Holy Spirit lead them in whatever kind of prayer he suggested. Paul was chiefly concerned with mental prayer and whatever vocal prayers were used were fine by him as long as they led to mental prayer. When he did suggest vocal prayers, as we have seen he did from time to time, he simply listed prayers and prayer attitudes that were customary at the time. For him the important thing was an inner attitude of communicating with God and listening to the Holy Spirit. That is why he ends this list of prayers to Agnes with the following recommendation, "If during these vocal prayers you should feel yourself drawn to mental prayer with deep recollection, let go the vocal prayers and enter into mental prayer. Then return to your vocal prayers. Give to each its time. Pray gently with your spirit in God" (I, 104).

In spite of this list of vocal prayers, Paul was not one for recommending long vocal prayers. He writes to Francis Appiani, "Don't burden yourself with too many vocal prayers. Those which you do say, say well. Make use of the help of ejaculatory prayers" (I, 418). He writes in the same way to Thomas Fossi, "Concerning vocal prayers, you know that I have already given you direction. Nevertheless, I also want to say that it is better to say a few good ones than many with little devotion" (I, 710).

Leaving Vocal Prayer

For Paul, vocal prayer was a stepping stone to mental prayer. He encouraged those he directed to move from vocal to mental prayer as soon as they felt the Holy Spirit drawing them in this direction. He says this to Agnes in the letter just quoted. He also writes to Teresa Palozzi, "When you are reciting vocal prayers and God draws your soul to the peace and quiet of interior recollection and you know that your spirit is remaining in God in a sacred silence of faith and love, leave off your vocal prayers and continue with mental prayer in that holy recollection of love in which your soul will be enriched with every good" (III, 374).

He also writes to her about confessors who would have her pray only vocal prayers and not go on to mental prayer. "If your confessors are persuading you to say vocal prayers, good. Vocal prayer is most holy, highly regarded by the Church. But when the soul is drawn to mental prayer and interior recollection, it is better to let the vocal prayers go and follow the breeze of the Holy Spirit. This is the teaching of spiritual masters and you know that I teach it too" (III, 383).

When we are praying set vocal prayers, we are more conscious of what we are doing than when we engage in mental prayer, especially if the Lord draws us to a quiet, recollected mental prayer. We might need some reassurance that we are on the right track. Paul always gave that reassurance to those under his direction.

Seeing God in Nature

For Paul, vocal prayers were an external help to the prayer of communication with God which took place interiorly, or as he loved to put it, quoting Jesus, "in spirit and in truth" (Jn 4:24). Another external help that Paul recommended was studying nature to hear what it said of God. He urges Francis Appiani to walk outside and hear what nature has to say. "Walk outside alone and listen to the preaching which is done by the flowers, the trees, the plants, the heavens and the whole world, and you will see that they are preaching sermons of love, of praise of God, and inviting you to praise and glorify this Sovereign Architect who gave them their being" (I, 418).

Paul loved nature and loved to look at and listen to the flowers and trees to hear what they were saying to him about God and to hear how God was talking to him through them. He recommended contemplating nature as one means of raising the mind and heart to God to enter into prayer-conversation with him. Paul also loved heights and panoramic views and wanted all his religious houses, as far as possible, to be built on mountains, hills, or elevated places to give a better view of nature and to make it easier to raise the vision of the heart to God.

Another of his loves was the sea. Many of his comparisons to our inner life with God are taken from the sea, both in its calmness and in its storms. In the years that he lived on Monte Argentario, he was not far from two fishing villages and often went there to minister to the fishermen and their families. It was only natural, then, that many of his analogies are taken from fishing, sailing and swimming. He spoke of the ocean of God's love, the Passion, and how we should fish for pearls in it. He spoke of swimming in the ocean of God's love. All these comparisons provided mental, and at times, vocal, images to use to bring his own heart and the hearts of those he directed to God.

Paul's primary concern in all of this was to bring the one he directed to inner communication with God. Whether this was done by vocal prayer, meditation, studying nature or whatever, it did not matter. What did matter was to use any means that would help to come to repose in God or, to use his own favorite metaphor, to rest on the bosom of God.

CHAPTER 10

The Bosom of God

One expression Paul frequently uses is "the bosom of God," or "drinking from the breasts of God." He draws many analogies and lessons from this simple comparison with a baby at its mother's breast. Paul uses these expressions so frequently that we cannot ignore them and still be faithful to his thoughts on spiritual direction. Let us take a look at some of these.

God's Will

The most fundamental comparison is the acceptance of God's will. Paul writes to Nicolina Martinez, "Abandon yourself always more on the loving bosom of our dear God, not being afraid of aridity or desolations or anything else, but with a strong heart press on. Oh, how much it pleases his divine Majesty when we lovingly abandon our will into his" (I, 39).

Paul used the same basic comparison when he spoke of distractions, as we saw at the end of Chapter 6 on "The Passion in Our Lives," in speaking of drinking in the milk of holy love from God's breast. Our will, Paul says, is like a baby's mouth. As long as our will is on God's will, we drink in the milk of holy love. God is all love and we drink in his love by uniting our will to his. This surrender to God's will is basic to all Paul's spirituality, as we saw in Chapter 4.

Jesus himself could say, "My will is to do the will of the One Who sent me" (Jn 4:34). And also, "The One Who sent me is with me. He hasn't left me alone because I always do what's pleasing to him" (Jn 8:29). For Jesus, the two statements were the same. We open the mouth of our will to God and he fills it with his love. Humanly speaking, the things he asks us to do or let be done to us often do not look like love since our love-vision is so blurred by our sinful nature. But Jesus accepted everything as love that his Father indicated to him as love, and Paul of the Cross did the same.

God's Constant Feeding

Paul draws another lesson from this image which does go beyond the capacity of a breast-feeding mother, who cannot be feeding her baby all the time as God can feed us. He writes to Mother Mary Crucified, "Remain day and night on the divine breast of the heavenly Father, clothed with Jesus Christ and his sufferings, and like a little baby, take in abundance the milk of holy love from the most holy breast of divine love" (II, 309). At least a breast-feeding mother usually does feed her baby in the middle of the night as well as during waking hours, and that served for Paul as a takeoff point for encouraging the awareness that we are constantly receiving God's nourishing love as long as our will is on him.

Freedom from Care

Another comparison Paul draws from the baby at the breast is the absence of care and anxiety. Babies do not have worries, and this is the way Paul wanted those he directed to be. He has another letter to Mother Mary Crucified in which he encourages her as usual and then urges her to let go of her anxieties even in suffering. "Live abandoned to his divine good pleasure in that desolate naked suffering in which you find yourself, without complaining either inwardly or outwardly to others. Rest like a baby on the breast of the heavenly Father, leaving to him the care of every event. Don't even think what will happen to yourself either in time or eternity, but suffer in the sacred silence of faith, naked, poor, annihilated on the cross of our gentle Jesus" (II, 293).

We are accustomed to think of babies as being relaxed and at peace on their mother's breast, but when they are uncomfortable they are not that way. Yet Paul believed that for those who were faithful to God, his Holy Spirit would give that peace and freedom from care which we see in a relaxed baby, and that this would continue even in the midst of trials and crosses. This peace is given by the Spirit to those who are open to it. It is not a skill acquired by straining our muscles or by making any kind of heroic efforts. If we think of suffering in silence and peace, we can easily get discouraged. But Paul knew by experience that for those who are faithful, the Spirit gives this attitude of silent willingness for suffering and deep inner peace without straining mind or heart; Jesus speaks of this when leaving his followers at the Last Supper. He says, "Peace I leave with you; my peace I give to you; not as the world gives do I give to you" (Jn 14:27). The world can give peace only by making the outward situation calm (if even this is possible). Jesus is able and wants to give us deep peace inside so that we can have it even when the outward situation is not calm but troubled and painful.

Paul wrote eloquently on this point. Listen to this letter: "A thousand times fortunate is the soul if, espoused to the divine will, it caresses this sovereign spouse in naked suffering within and without, reposing on the breast of the heavenly Father and being nourished in spirit and in truth by the heavenly manna of the divine will, tasting and relishing that it should be accomplished in every event, no matter how bitter it may be. When it looks with the eye of faith on the greatest trials, storms and afflictions of spirit and of body, when it looks at them, I say, with the eye of faith, as joys flowing from the breast of holy love, they are no longer bitter but most sweet and delightful!" (II, 291).

Statements like this can easily sound exaggerated to our modern ears, since most of us have never experienced anything like what Paul is describing. But this description is Paul's own experience and what he believed the Lord would do for all who fully surrendered themselves to his good pleasure. Many other saints have said the same. St. Thérèse of Lisieux, the Little Flower, wrote to her sister Celine when she was only sixteen, "Let us not expect to find love without suffering." (Letters, April 26, 1889). And she also said that if she had not experienced what joy God could give in suffering for him, she would not have believed it. Most of us are not that fully surrendered to God's will that we experience the joy he wants to give us, even in suffering, but if we keep going ahead in faith, we are assured by the saints that it will come eventually. However, if we are looking for the joy and not simply to please God, we have already defeated ourselves.

Drink from the Passion

For Paul, drinking from the breast of God was the same as drinking from the open side of Jesus on the cross. Paul frequently speaks of drinking the mixture of love and suffering. He believed that God would draw to that experience those who were faithful. He counseled that in prayer, if the attraction to just be with God was felt, it was from the Spirit and at that point the communication between God and the soul would be very deep. He writes to Agnes Grazi, "When your soul experiences a relish in being one on one with God, with a pure and loving attention to God in simple faith, reposing on the most sweet breast of its Beloved Good in a sacred silence of love, let it be this way. The soul speaks to God more this way than if it were using words because then God carries it in his arms" (I, 113).

Attention to Practicalities

It might seem when Paul recommends to lay people, busy with the daily cares of a family, to lose themselves in divine contemplation, that if they did such a thing they would be living in another world from their families and not be able to fulfill their daily responsibilities. Paul did not see it that way. He believed that the closer one drew to God, the better able he or she would be to take care of other daily duties. The Spirit would lead them in this regard too.

Paul writes to Thomas Fossi, "All your desire should be to please God and to live abandoned like a baby into the arms of his divine will. When you do this, your monastery or retreat will be your own interior in which your spirit should remain alone and hidden in the bosom of God, living a divine life, a life of love, a holy life, being born every moment in the divine Word, Christ, our Lord. This will happen if you remain in your nothingness and solitude in the inner temple of your spirit. This divine solitude will not be impeded by your other interests nor by the care of your house and children nor by anything else that your place in life requires. These are obligations of justice. When you fulfill them faithfully you will be even more pleasing to the Lord" (I, 641).

Paul himself was a very practical man. He was a great mystic, but great mystics are not what is often thought — dreamy unrealists. They are very much in touch with the problems of everyday life and especially with the needs of others. Paul advocated complete dedication to a life of prayer, hut never in such a way that it would make anyone incapable of being aware of the needs of those around them and of fulfilling whatever obligations they had in daily life.

Paul believed that the more one was attuned to the Holy Spirit, the more the Spirit would remind them of their daily duties and give them the light and strength to fulfill them. The words of Jesus fit well here with the work of the Spirit in this regard. "The Holy Spirit whom the Father will send in my name, will teach you everything and will remind you of all the things I told you" (Jn 14:26). Paul trusted that the Holy Spirit would always bring to our minds whatever we need to think of at the moment. He can think of us even when we cannot think of him. If we remain on the breast of God, we will always know what to do.

CHAPTER II

Recollection

aul of the Cross took the biblical recommendation, "Pray constantly" (1 Th 5:17), literally and seriously. He himself wanted to pray at all times and to have those he directed to do the same. He wanted this even when daily duties and responsibilities would not allow focusing the mind on God as would be possible when there was time free from other occupations. But busy or not, Paul wanted those he directed to be engaged in constant prayer, or, as it is often called, recollection.

He writes to Sister Cherubina Bresciani, "When you are at peace in God in a sacred silence of love, with a pure but gentle attention of love to God in living faith, you are praying with a prayer that lasts 24 hours a day, because you are always in the presence of God, adoring him in spirit and in truth (Jn 4:24)" (I, 443).

Attention of Heart

For Paul, this constant attention to God was an attention of the heart, not of the mind. It did not mean that a recollected person would be oblivious to what was going on round about. Just the opposite. He writes to Thomas Fossi, "If you remain in the inner temple of your spirit, this divine solitude will not keep you from taking care of your family and fulfilling the other duties of your life. These are your responsibilities and fulfilling them faithfully is what is always more pleasing to God" (I, 641).

In another letter he expresses it this way to Thomas, "When you are entirely recollected and abandoned into the bosom of the heavenly Father, adoring him in spirit and in truth, such recollection does not take away from you the attention you owe to your domestic affairs, but enables you to take care of them with greater diligence and perfection, since your work will be entirely perfumed with the balm of holy love" (I, 592).

Paul, in accord with most spiritual masters, did not see recollection as depending on the attention of the intellect, but on focusing the heart, or will, on God. He saw the acceptance of God's will as the key to open the door of recollection and to receive it as a gift from God. As he puts it in a letter to one of his own priests, "When we seek in all things the divine good pleasure, and keep ourselves in true fidelity and complete resignation to the divine will, keeping our interior well regulated, quiet, serene, detached from all created things, so that we can be a delight to Jesus Christ, we dispose ourselves always more for the gift of recollection to become continuous adorers of the Most High in spirit and in truth" (III, 340).

Paul wanted those he directed to be recollected at all times, but yet, as we have just seen from his letter to that priest, he recognized such recollection as a gift from God. Therefore he was opposed to all efforts to force recollection, as if it could be gained by strenuous human efforts. He writes to Thomas, "Without forcing your mind in the matter, gently keep your holy recollection and attend to the duties of your house since this is what the Lord desires of you" (I, 752). And in another place, "Keep your heart recollected, but without forcing your mind" (I, 546).

Peace: the Sign of Recollection

The sign of such recollection, as Paul saw it, was inner peace. He writes to Thomas, "Don't let your heart become agitated by anxieties, but keep it always peaceful and in loving repose on the bosom of God. Don't will anything else other than what his divine Majesty wills. No matter what kind of adversities arise, whether within or without, be at peace and in silence with a 'Your will be done' [Mk 14:36]. Then proceed to sleep on the cross in the warmth of the loving heart of Jesus." (I, 728)

However, we do know that anxieties will arise, and Paul knew it too. What do we do when they come? He writes, "Remain in pure faith and holy love in the most intimate chamber of your spirit, in your inner depths. Repose gently on the loving bosom of your Beloved Good in sacred silence, in interior nudity and inner solitude. When your occupations seem to make you lose somewhat the gentle vision of the Supreme Good, arouse yourself with gentle aspirations, brief, yet penetrating, keeping the sacred fire of divine love always kindled on the altar of your heart. Place there the bundle of aromatic logs which are the mysteries of the most holy life, Passion, and death of Jesus Christ. All this can take place in a moment, in faith and holy love, without great reflections or long discourses" (I, 567).

Paul believed that if the heart was at peace it was recollected, no matter what else might be going on. The busiest occupations could not disturb recollection if there were peace in the heart. In fact, Paul advised Thomas not to be too introspective and not to try to look inside closely to see if he were recollected or not. He was to simply be at peace. "Work in peace and without curiosity of spirit; that is, don't go around looking to see how well this most noble work which his divine Majesty is doing in your soul by means of holy recollection is coming along. Simply keep on going" (I, 567).

Learning From Disturbances

In other words, we don't have to keep examining ourselves to see if we are recollected. If we are inwardly at peace, we are recollected or peace would not be there. If we find ourselves anxious and upset in any way, then we need to do something about it to return to inner peace. Anxieties and inner disturbances usually come from inner attitudes of heart, past programming, past hurts and past habits which are not totally conformed to God's holy will, past habits which have developed from that programming, and past hurts which have not been worked through to peace. They are like God's messages to us telling us we need to do something. They are like a telephone bell ringing to disturb our peace so that we will listen to God in some area where we are not yet fully conformed to his will. Since these areas are usually crosses of some type to us, that is why Paul urges Thomas to make brief darts of his thoughts to the Passion of Jesus to regain his inner peace.

For example, suppose your car breaks down on the highway (obviously this is not an example Paul would have used) and you find yourself inwardly tense as you are trying to size up the situation to see what you can do about it. Paul would recommend that you think of the Passion of Jesus until you come to inner peace. Our natural tendency in such a situation is simply to let our human feelings act as they have been faultily programmed to act our whole past life. We don't immediately look at such a situation in the light of faith as a purifying cross that the Lord is sending us. We don't see truth until we see things in the light of faith. As we come to do this with more and more ease, we come to a deeper and deeper recollection in the events of daily life, even and perhaps especially in the unpleasant ones.

Constant Recollection

Paul believed that inner recollection was possible (by the grace of God, not by our own efforts) in all situations. He puts it this way, "Remain in peaceful interior solitude in pure faith and holy love, reposing on the bosom of the heavenly Father. There you will find every good. You can experience this solitude in all situations, in every event, without breaking your head or your mind, by a gentle, loving attention, arousing and reviving your faith in a gentle and peaceful way in the superior part, which is the most noble section, or sanctuary, of the soul" (I, 580).

Paul did not consider turmoil in our feelings, or what he would call theologically the lower part of the soul, as disturbances to our recollection. He would see them rather as a call from God to a deeper recollection as he gave these feelings to the Lord that he might calm and heal whatever in them needed healing at the moment. In this part of the soul are included our fears, repugnances, desires, impulses, annoyances, resentments, temper flare-ups, and so forth. The superior part of the soul is the mind and heart, the intellect and the free will, or power of choice. It is chiefly in the superior part that we are recollected and united with God, and it is with these faculties of our soul that we love, even though we may not feel that we are loving.

Many people who are trying to lead a life of love of God become disturbed when they find that they do not often think explicitly of God during the day. Paul would not consider this a problem. For him the important thing was not whether they had explicit thoughts of God or any thought of God, but whether God was thinking of them. Of course, God is always thinking of us and always loving us — always communicating to us his holy will in each situation. As long as we are receiving this communication, we are at peace, and this, for Paul, was the important sign. If we are upset and agitated it is like static in the line of communication, that partially at least, disturbs our reception of what God is communicating to us. It does not mean that we are no longer recollected, but that there are "loose wires" in our communication system which we have to ask the Lord to fix. Since we are all born with faulty communication systems and many "loose wires," we are bound to be upset from time to time. But each time this happens and we allow the Lord to heal it, our communication system is improved and our recollection deepens.

For example, suppose we have to wait in a dentist's office and the dentist is late for the appointment. We may find ourselves getting tense and nervous. Paul would recommend turning to the Passion of Jesus. As we have seen before, the sufferings of life are an invitation from God to enter more deeply into the Passion of Jesus. One of the sufferings of life in this situation would be the cross of waiting. None of us naturally likes to wait. We would prefer to have everything happen without waiting for it, and that it would be under our control. When we have to wait, things are not under our control and we need to leave them in God's hands.

During his Passion, Jesus had to accept the cross of waiting — waiting for daybreak for his trial, for example. We need to learn to choose for ourselves what Jesus chose for himself, and his must be our constant attitude of heart even though not always of our feelings. Once we see that we are subconsciously resisting something God wants of us, such as waiting in the dentist's office, then with the gentle help of God's grace we can change our attitude and become willing to wait. As we do this in more and more situations, we find that our willingness to wait grows and we become less and less tense when we have to wait for something. In this way we become more and more recollected.

Recollection When at Fault

One situation in which it is difficult to keep our recollection and remain at peace is when we notice some fault or defect in ourselves. It seems that we are programmed to presume that God loves us only because we are good, or only when we are good, like a child trying to be good in December so that Santa Claus will bring him the presents he wants. We do not easily come to peace in accepting ourselves especially with our faults. Only slowly do we grow in awareness that our faults do not in the least lessen God's love for us. Paul writes to Sister Cherubina Bresciani, "Remain in the divine bosom of the Supreme Good; keep your inner peace. Flee disturbances as a plague and don't even let yourself be disturbed by your own faults. Humble yourself before God with a gentle and loving sorrow and a willingness to change. Then go on in peace without losing your inner solitude" (I, 301).

It is never easy to accept a particular fault in ourselves, but such acceptance is especially difficult when we had not noticed that defect in ourselves for a long time and had presumed we had overcome it. When there are no manifestations of that shortcoming for a long time, and then we fall into it again, it is easy to become discouraged. How often have we said, or heard others say, "I thought I was beyond that." Famous last words! In this situation we need something of the attitude of St. Thérèse, the Little Flower, who could discover impatience in herself even on her deathbed without becoming discouraged. We all need to be able to take our faults in stride, and yet keep our peace and recollection.

Another situation in which it is hard to remain recollected, or rather, hard to believe that we are still recollected, is when we lose the sense, the feeling, of God's presence. When we are beginners in walking the way of the Lord, he ordinarily gives us many signs of his presence and many wonderful feelings when we pray, take part in the liturgy, go on retreats, take part in spiritual gatherings, and so forth. As we walk farther along the way of the Lord, these feelings usually leave us.

The feeling of God is not God, and he has to teach us to seek himself alone and not just our own pleasant feelings. When this happens, it is so easy to presume that God is displeased with us and that we are going backward rather than forward in the spiritual life. It is not easy at such times to believe that we are still recollected. Paul writes to Mother Mary Crucified who was having precisely that problem, "Continue to be interiorly recollected. There is no aridity whatsoever that can prevent this. It is not important that you feel the taste of the divine presence. What is important is that you remain in pure faith, deprived of all contentment for the love of God, so that he may be the contentment of our contentment. Therefore remain in repose like a child on the breast of God, in a silence of faith and holy love with the superior part of your spirit, without paying any attention to the noises that these enemies are making within your spirit" (II, 301).

The apostles Peter, James, and John were so filled with wonderful sensations on the Mount of the Transfiguration that Peter wanted to camp there and continue to experience these ecstatic feelings (Mt 17:4). Later on in a similar prayer situation in Gethsemane, they had no such delightful feelings. They not only didn't want to set up any tents there, they ran like scared jackrabbits when trouble came. When the Lord reproved them for not being able to watch and pray with him (cf. Mk 14:37), the apostles probably felt they were going backward. Since that situation proved to be a valuable learning experience, they were doubtless going forward in God's eyes. The same fears that were with the three in Gethsemane had doubtless been hidden inside them on the Mount of the Transfiguration too, but the situation there did not activate these fears. They needed this new situation to surface those feelings. Then they could ask the Lord for healing. They had to have a healing of the tendency to let their fears control them so that they could be recollected even in painful situations.

We likewise have our delightful situations and our painful ones. We need to know that we are not regressing even though we notice more faults in painful situations than in pleasurable ones. We need to discover that when things get dry and dark, even as dark as Gethsemane, God is right there with us in the darkness. There may be no feeling of God, but God has not left us. We need to come to peace even in the darkness and know that we are still recollected and are still pleasing to God. Paul of the Cross went through all this himself and so was able to encourage others who felt that God had left them. He could reassure them as he can us, that as long as deep down inside ourselves we want and choose what God wants, even though we don't feel it, and don't want it by natural inclination, we are still in fact recollected.

CHAPTER 12

Penances

There are many helps to a life of prayer. One of the chief helps Paul speaks of is penance — the performance or acceptance of penances. In the eighteenth century it was presumed that anyone who wanted to live a life of prayer and union with God should perform many external penances: much fasting, use of the discipline, wearing chains, and so forth. The discipline was a little whip made of cords or chains with which one afflicted oneself to cause bodily pain in honor of the scourging of Jesus. Chains were worn around the waist which had little points on them to cut into the skin. Many other such afflictive devices were also used.

Paul himself used many of these instruments of penance even in public when giving missions, since that was the custom of the time. He had his own ideas on penance, as we shall see, hut outwardly he conformed to the practices of the time and more or less took them for granted.

However, in his direction of others, Paul did not conform to the expected ideas of the time. He was often asked about particular penances, since it was also the custom of that day and age to get permission from one's confessor or spiritual director for the performance of any penance. Paul's approach was more or less to go along with what was customary, but the principles he gave were very different from those of his time — and even very different from the practice of external penances by many today.

God's Penances

For one thing, we never find Paul urging anyone to perform more penances than they were actually doing. On the contrary, he was forever mitigating them for one reason or other. Paul never considered external penances as necessary for holiness. What he considered essential were what he called God's penances: the trials and afflictions that are part of daily living. As we have already considered, Paul saw all troubles as coming from the loving hand of God. Accepting these willingly was what Paul never ceased urging.

For example, he wrote to Agnes Grazi, "When you are sick in bed or are taking medicine, leave off the little chains and take the penance God is giving you" (I, 155). By the penances God was giving, Paul meant the sickness itself and also the unpleasant medicines and other remedies that are often necessary to cure the sickness.

Paul also writes to Agnes, "If your pains continue, lighten your penances. In this I leave you free to do as you judge you should. But the truth is that when the body is doing that penance which God gives it, it is necessary to lessen the penances we pick ourselves" (I, 217).

In comparing the two kinds of penances, those we pick ourselves and those God picks for us, Paul had no doubt as to which was to be preferred. He writes to Thomas Fossi, "Concerning penances, for the moment you must content yourself with those that God gives. These are infinitely better than those we impose on ourselves" (I, 542). Infinitely better. That was Paul's conviction in the matter. We are often more inclined to those we pick ourselves. But we need to become more attuned to what God is doing in and with us.

In this same vein Paul writes again to Thomas, "Be discreet in your penances. Accept the penances God gives you" (I, 648). Paul gives the reason why he considered that penances sent by God are better than those we pick ourselves. He expresses it this way: "Be content with your pains and other discomforts. These are more pleasing to God than all your voluntary self-chosen penances, since there is nothing of self in them" (I, 543). Even in penance there can often be a secret pride. The human tendency is to pick the penances that will look best on our record. But the penances God sends are often humiliating and we would never pick them ourselves. For this reason they are much more powerful to destroy the pride and selfishness within us.

Examples of God's Penances

Paul gives some examples of what he calls "God's penances." He writes to Thomas, "See to it that your penances are a continuous exercise of virtues: humility of heart, mortification of your passions, bearing with adversity, sweetness and love towards others, resignation to the will of God, recollection of heart, remembering the Passion of Jesus, frequenting the sacraments and (here is an excellent one for parents) the careful education of your children" (I, 562). Perhaps seeing to it that your children do their homework is a penance far better than a year's worth of fasting!

Another penance Paul mentions for those who devote themselves to prayer is the dryness and prolonged aridity that are often experienced. "Concerning aridity and other desolations which are experienced both in Holy Communion and other spiritual pursuits, these are a means God uses to strip you of self-love and to dispose you for great graces" (I, 453).

Two other penances Paul mentions in this regard are temperance and moderation. He writes, "For the present you have no need of great fasts, since life itself is giving you a beating. Temperance and moderation are a continuous fast" (I, 548). Temperance means controlling our appetites in eating and drinking. Anyone who has ever been on a diet knows how hard this is. Moderation means curbing one's impulsiveness. This, too, is a powerful penance.

Paul gives other examples. He writes to Thomas, "Be at peace in the trials that come up in your home, in events, in misfortunes, in too many mouths to feed, and so forth" (I, 528). Paul quotes the Second Letter to Timothy (3:12) and broadens its application: "In fact everyone who desires to live a holy life in Christ Jesus will suffer persecution." Paul adds to these words of the sacred writer, "By the words 'will suffer persecution' are understood all sorts of trials, from the devil or from men, or from our own rebellious flesh, and so on" (II, 115). He adds to the list in writing to Mother Mary Crucified, "the disapproval of relatives and others, afflictions, fears, desolation, aridity, abandonment, temptations and other persecutions" (II,309). In short, anything that we find unpleasant, Paul would call a penance coming from the loving hand of God. He would consider everything from pinpricks to hurricanes as penances from God, even though at times, they might be our own fault.

Attitude Towards Penances

The important thing for him was not what the particular penance or cross was, or how big or little it was, but what was the attitude we had towards it. He wanted the same attitude that Jesus had towards his Passion — "The Son of Man had to suffer greatly" (Mk 8:31) — an attitude he repeated later on to the two disciples on the road to Emmaus (Lk 24:26). In other words, Paul wanted those he directed to see their trials as necessary. He did not want them to consider their trials as if they shouldn't be there, or as if God didn't want them, or as if they came from Satan without God's permission. Paul did not have the problem that so many have today when they say, "If God allows these things to happen, how can he love us." For Paul, God not only allowed, but sent these trials, but with love. Paul was well aware, as so many today are not, that trials are necessary.

Paul writes to Sister Columba Gandolfi, "You must realize that to reach a great union with God by way of holy love, trials are necessary" (II, 448). He then goes on to console her by reassuring her that God is right with her in all trials, hidden within, and is holding her tightly in his arms.

Paul quotes the words of the Archangel Raphael to Tobiah according to the Vulgate version, "Because you were acceptable to God, it was necessary that trials purify you [Tb 12:13]" (I, 570). Paul goes on to add, "Note the words necessary and trials, meaning all sorts of trials." He always wanted to make it quite clear to those he directed that every trial God sends is necessary or he would not send it.

Once we have understood that such trials and God-given penances are necessary, then it follows that we need to accept them as best we can. He writes to Mother Mary Crucified, "Be dead and buried in the divine good pleasure without complaining about anything, but take every suffering without looking at the intermediary, directly from the loving hand of the Supreme Good, who can only will what is best for you" (II, 312).

Fruits of Penance

Only God knows why he does things. But Paul could see some of the fruits of penance and he mentions some of these fruits for the encouragement of those who were being tried. He writes to Father Fulgentius, one of his own Passionist priests, "How I wish we would attract interior men who would know how to be constant in suffering the afflictions, the pressures, and the inner trials which are so necessary to purify the spirit so that at every moment it might be renewed in its divine birth in Christ Jesus in the most pure faith and holy love!" (II,

150).

Paul writes to Lucy Burlini, "By means of your sufferings, even the imperfections you are not aware of are being purified and your soul is becoming like a crystal reflecting the light of the divine Sun and you will become entirely transformed in God through love" (II,719). We all have faults within us that we do not see, even though others may be aware of them. Many of the trials God sends help these faults to surface, so that we can present them to him for healing. But often, too, God heals them directly by the trials he sends without our even being conscious of what has been happening. If we trust him and let him do what he wants with us, far more good things happen than we could ever realize in this lifetime.

The greatest result of all these penances and trials is love of God. The trials God sends both purify and develop our love. Paul writes to Agnes Grazi, "Don't be surprised that after the fiercest storms of temptation the soul is accustomed to remain more peaceful and more in love with God" (I, 238). Paul wanted those he directed not merely to love God in a general sort of way, hut to really be in love with him, intensely and passionately, as he himself was. For Paul, this was the great result of all penance and all suffering.

Connecting Penance with Love

To accept penances and sufferings with this motivation, though, it is necessary first to realize that we are loved. That was why Paul connected all this with looking at Jesus' sufferings, hearing his love and responding. Paul quotes to Agnes words he had heard from Jesus, "He who embraces me, embraces thorns.' Just as Jesus wanted to live his most holy life on earth in the midst of suffering, trial, fatigue, privation, anguish, scorn, calumny, sorrow, blows, nails, thorns and the most bitter death of the cross, so he made me understand that, embracing him, I must lead a life of suffering! And oh, with what joy my poor soul embraced every kind of suffering!" (I, 194). Paul believed that suffering, fully accepted from God, would bring joy. He believed it was not suffering itself that was the problem for us; it was the refusal of suffering. He quotes the Letter of James, "Consider it a cause for joy whenever you encounter various trials [1:2]" (II, 704).

For Paul of the Cross, it was not so much suffering that brought joy, but love — even when there was suffering with the beloved. He believed that if we aim at love, all our needs of a penitential nature will be taken care of. He said this especially to those who were sick or infirm and not able to do the penances that the culture of the times expected of them. But the principle of putting love first is true of all times and all cultures. As St. Thérèse, the Little Flower, was to put it a century later, "Love is the greatest penance."

CHAPTER 13

Other Spiritual Helps

esides penances, there were other helps to a life of prayer and union with God that Paul spoke of. He frequently spoke of Confession and Communion referring to them in the way that was usual at the time as "the Sacraments." There are other Sacraments, of course, but these were the only two to which people had frequent access. Besides the Sacraments, he spoke also of the reading of spiritual books, especially the Sacred Scriptures, and of making retreats. These we will consider in this chapter, beginning with Communion.

Communion

Today in our Catholic culture, it is becoming more and more common that those who go to Mass go to Communion. Communion is considered a normal part of the Mass, not an exceptional practice. It can be easy to forget that this has not been the case for very long and that it was far from being the case in Paul's culture. We do not find those Paul directed being urged by him to go to Mass, since presumably they were already going as often as they could. But we do find him urging them to go to Communion frequently, since frequent Communion was not the custom of the time. In fact, even cloistered nuns had to be urged at times to go at least once a month. Weekly and especially daily Communion was a rarity. Those who did go often were likely to be looked down on as ostentatiously flaunting their holiness.

In this climate we find Paul going contrary to his culture and recommending frequent Communion, even daily when possible. Paul writes to Agnes Grazi, "Regarding Communion, go on all feast days and even three times every week. During Passiontide, from Passion Sunday to Holy Thursday, go every day if you can" (I, 109). He also tells her that she doesn't have to go to confession every time, since many thought then, and some still do today, that this was necessary.

At another time after recommending to her to communicate every Sunday, Wednesday and Friday and on feasts, he suggests that on the other days she make a spiritual Communion (I, 212). This consisted in a desire of the heart to be inwardly united to Jesus and could be made several times a day. In today's situation, with the removal of restrictions on the frequency of Communion, spiritual Communions are rarely mentioned. However, it may well be that the expressed desire for union with Jesus is something which is much more common today, though it is not called spiritual Communion.

To Thomas Fossi Paul recommends going to Communion every week (I, 572). To a cloistered nun he writes, "When you have the good fortune to have the opportunity to go to Communion and your confessor lets you, go every time" (III, 342). In those days it was customary to get permission from one's confessor to go to Communion. It is hard for us today to imagine such a situation.

Perhaps one reason why people thought they had to go to Confession every time they went to Communion was to get this permission. Also Confession and Communion were commonly spoken of in those days as a unit and called simply, "the Sacraments." Paul writes to his own brothers and sisters, "Frequently approach the Sacraments, that is Holy Confession and Most Holy Communion" (I, 53). However, Paul adds here as he often does, a reason to make use of the Sacraments, especially Communion, "to maintain divine friendship and that your souls may be liquified in the fire of his most holy love."

Today when we speak of assisting at Mass or participating in the liturgy we usually assume we will receive Communion, rather than speaking of Communion as a separate issue. But the Council of Trent, two centuries before Paul's time, had issued a decree on the Mass and only after fifteen years or more issued a decree on Communion. For this reason, theology manuals and catechisms even up to today have usually treated Communion separately from the Mass. Paul did the same and more or less presumed the Mass while speaking mostly about Communion. In this, he was probably more in line with our ancient biblical tradition which speaks of what we call the Mass as the "breaking of the bread," implying Communion.

Fruits of Communion

Paul was convinced of the power of Communion to fire the heart with love. As we have just quoted in his letter to his own family, he speaks of Communion as liquifying the heart in God's love. Paul did not consider going to Communion as a reward for virtue (as was frequently done at the time) but as a power to intensify love in the heart by communication with the love of Christ Himself. He writes to Agnes, "Never cease embracing him in the great Sacrament of his love. Let go of the bridle of your heart to give free rein to your affections with this infinite love. Leave yourself free to aspire to that glory which has been prepared for you by the infinite merits of Jesus" (I, 238).

For Paul, the chief meaning of Communion was love and its chief effect was love. He did not question the manner or style of going to Communion, which was very different in his day from what it is today, and certainly very different from what it was in the early Church. But he saw it as a power to intensify love in the heart by union with Jesus and to fill the heart with all the virtues that are needed for love to grow.

Paul wanted those he directed to open their hearts to the totality of the fire of love which he himself found in this Sacrament. He wrote to Sister Colomba Gandolfi, "I beg you and strongly beg you not to omit Communion. Oh my daughter! Never omit this food of eternal life and treat with him in long thanksgivings in the manner and form in which he will guide you and teach you" (II, 459). Paul saw Communion as real communion, which to him meant love-union with Jesus.

He could become eloquent on the value of Communion and its love-purpose. In the letter to his brothers and sisters he writes, "Oh, my dear ones! I do not speak to you of preparation for Communion, since I know you do all you can. Our dear Jesus could do nothing greater than to give himself as our food. Therefore let us love this dear Lover, and be greatly devoted to the Most Blessed Sacrament" (I, 54).

Paul could easily explain the love-union with God that Communion brought about, since he himself experienced it. He did not explain the union with one another which can be a fruit of Communion, since at his time Communion (and Mass) was strictly a private affair. Even if the church was full, the people did not share with one another. Their only external participation was to stand, sit and kneel at the same time. As a result there was not much human awareness of one another and the focus of devout people was on God within them. They were aware, as Paul certainly was that they were to love one another as Christians and that Communion was a great help. But there was no human external sign of this, so that aspect of Communion was not developed at the time. It remained for later centuries to do this.

Sacrament of Penance

The other Sacrament which was included in the commonly used expression "the Sacraments" was the Sacrament of Penance or Confession, today usually called the Sacrament of Reconciliation. At Paul's time the strong emphasis was on this Sacrament as a ritual in which God's forgiveness was obtained. Who the priest was did not matter all that much, whether he was learned or ignorant, skilled in dealing with people or unskilled, amiable or cantankerous. Paul speaks of both good and bad confessors.

He writes to Agnes, "I am supremely happy that you have found a good Confessor. God knows how consoled I am" (I, 106). At the same time, he could write in the opposite vein to Mother Mary Crucified, "I am happy to hear that this new confessor treats you sharply and is hard and severe. What a good friend he is" (II, 301). It might seem as if Paul is talking out of both sides of his mouth but he was speaking of something different each time. In speaking to Agnes, he was referring to the normal course of events in which it is a grace to find a good confessor. In writing to Mother Mary Crucified Paul went on to explain that God was using this confessor as a chisel to shape her into the beautiful statue God wanted her to become. Having had to deal with both kinds of confessors himself in his younger years, Paul knew how to draw profit from both.

Just as he advocated frequent Communion, so did Paul advocate frequent Confession. In writing to a married woman, Paul recommends that she go to Confession once a week (III, 814). But in this case he himself was the confessor so we can he sure he did not allow her to become scrupulous about it. The emphasis in those days was on the grace the Sacrament produced by the ritual itself, and it was presumed that the more often one went, the better. For someone who went to Confession to Paul, this was probably true. But for someone who went to a poorly qualified confessor, this might be called into question. Paul never questioned this practice. It was one of the devotional assumptions of the time that no one seemed to question.

Confession and Spiritual Direction

However, it is important to note that for Paul, Confession and spiritual direction were not the same. Confession deals chiefly with the acknowledgment of sins or faults, and hopefully receiving from the confessor some advice on seeking the causes of these faults. One would hope that it would also include receiving from the confessor some advice on seeking the causes of these faults in our own hidden inner attitudes which are not the same as the attitudes of Christ. Spiritual direction is chiefly concerned with growth in a life of prayer, understanding better the working of the Holy Spirit and living one's whole life under his guidance.

Sometimes Paul exercised both functions, hut not usually. The ones he wrote to ordinarily considered him their spiritual director, but had someone else nearby for a confessor. This is often the case today, too, with someone who has a spiritual director at a distance and a confessor close at hand. One reason Paul could write to Mother Mary Crucified that a severe confessor could be an instrument in God's hands for her purification, was that the confessor was not her spiritual director. Confession and spiritual direction can be joined, but not necessarily so. This is especially true today when many lay men and women are trained in spiritual direction. Paul himself was a spiritual director several years before he became a priest and could hear confessions. Paul would certainly agree that the important thing was not whether or not the spiritual director was a priest, but whether or not the director, priest or lay person, was competent.

Paul considers the Sacraments in his letters, not chiefly to give a treatise, or any part of one, on the theology of the Sacraments, but to see them in their role as helps in the inner life of union with God. He writes to one woman of the "palace of perfection" (a takeoff from Teresa of Avila's "Interior Castle" which Paul knew well). He speaks of the qualities she needed to build this, or as he corrects himself, to cooperate as God built it in her. Then he goes on to say, "But this cannot happen unless you are strong, and for this you need to be fed often by prayer, by the most holy Sacraments and by spiritual reading" (II, 5). Paul has volumes to say on prayer, and as we have seen, he speaks of the Sacraments (meaning Confession and Communion), only in relation to the life of God within. He rarely mentions reading, probably because many of those he directed could not read. But he does have some beautiful things to say about the Scriptures.

Reading the Scriptures

He writes to Thomas Fossi, who was worried that some seemed to approve of him and others didn't. Paul turns to the Scriptures for light on how to handle Thomas's problem in the light of how Jesus handled similar situations in His own life. But in using the Scriptures in this particular case, Paul gives his opinion on the value of all Scripture for the Christian life. "We have the Sacred Scriptures from which all theologians and moralists and mystics and dogmaticians and apologists have drawn their work. They have approved or disapproved of spirits according as these spirits were in conformity or not in conformity with what God has deigned to reveal and manifest in the Sacred Scriptures" (I, 819).

Thomas was an educated man and obviously used the Scriptures. Paul could encourage him in the use of the Bible. However, most of those Paul wrote to either could not read, as we have noted before, or did not possess a Bible. The reading of Scripture was not encouraged at that time for fear of private interpretation. It was presumed that private interpretation was the root of Protestantism and in those days there was no dialogue to understand Protestants, but simply unreasoning fear. Paul himself was thoroughly familiar with the Scriptures as his constant references to Scripture shows, but those he wrote to were not. In today's climate, where the Scriptures are widely read and used by Catholics, it would have been possible for Paul to make much more use of them for spiritual direction. However, the Holy Spirit is not limited by anything, not even the Bible, and our faith is not in the printed word, but in a person ,Jesus Christ. Paul knew and loved him and this was the basis of all his direction.

Making Retreats

One other help for a life of inner union with God which Paul recommends was the making of retreats. He writes to a priest in Rome, who had written to him speaking of the need to make a retreat. "I have read your letter in which you speak of your need to make a retreat of some days to free yourself from the turmoil of interests which do not fit your state, and from inner restlessness, so that you can recognize with a peaceful spirit that which his divine Majesty is moving you to do in order to accomplish his most holy will" (III, 721). Paul was highly in favor of this and affirmed the priest's intention.

Retreats to lay persons were not widespread at that time though Paul himself wanted a house on the grounds of his religious houses where lay people could come for the spiritual exercises for several days. This did not happen in his lifetime but it did after his death. In the United States, most of the larger Passionist houses have retreat houses attached to them.

However, even in Paul's time there were some lay persons who did go away for retreats. Writing to a layman, Paul recommends the spiritual exercises (another name for retreats) at least once a year. He mentions the Novitiate of the Jesuits in Rome as one place where this could be done (II,387). Future generations would see the development of retreat houses for lay people and the fulfillment of Paul's desire that retreats be available to all.

CHAPTER 14

Role of the Director

We have already spoken of Paul as spiritual director, but now let us look more closely at some of the things Paul believed and recommended regarding spiritual direction, both for the one under guidance and for the director himself. Today, we might add "or herself," but in Paul's time it almost never happened that a woman was a spiritual director.

Need for Spiritual Direction

Paul believed firmly in spiritual direction and believed that this was God's will for those who were seeking to lead a truly dedicated Christian life. He wrote to one of his own priests, "It pleases God that we walk with direction. 'Go to Ananias' [Ac 9:6], the great Divine Master said to St. Paul" (III, 704). The text quoted refers to the conversion of St. Paul the apostle and what Jesus said to him in vision. This text does not explicitly refer to spiritual direction as such, but it does imply that the Lord usually uses other people to give us lights from God and to help us understand our own. Paul of the Cross caught this implication and used it in many ways in his own life. He considered spiritual direction a normal need for anyone trying to lead a deep interior life.

In this he was in line with all the great masters of the spiritual life. St. Teresa of Avila, after she had founded the reformed branch of the Carmelite Nuns, then proceeded to found a reformed branch of the Carmelite Friars so that she would have spiritual directors for her nuns. God certainly can give each of us lights directly without any intermediary and he often does. But Jesus began his community, which we call the Church, as a body in which the members would need one another. Most of those who achieved great holiness, as far as we can tell, were helped by the direction of another. St. Teresa believed that many could be led to sanctity if only they were well directed. Yet God can give direction in any way he chooses and does give it directly at times.

God is the Chief Director

A good example of the contrast between God's two ways of acting is found in the lives of the two Teresas, St. Teresa of Avila and her spiritual daughter, St. Thérèse of Lisieux, better known as the Little Flower. Teresa of Avila had the unique privilege of having three canonized saints among her spiritual directors: St. John of the Cross, a Carmelite, St. Peter of Alcantara, a Franciscan, and St. Francis Borgia, a Jesuit. On the other hand, St. Thérèse received almost no spiritual direction in her life, even though she valued it highly and sought it as best she could. But the Lord consoled her with the words of Scripture concerning the Israelites in the desert after passing through the Red Sea: "He found them in a wilderness, a wasteland of howling desert. He shielded them and cared for them, guarding them as the apple of his eye. As an eagle incites its nestlings forth by hovering over its brood, so he spread his wings to receive them and bore them up on his pinions. The Lord alone was their leader" (Dt 32:10-12). She saw her absence of direction as a desert and this text gave her the comfort that God was there and loved her and would lead her where she needed to go.

God wants us to seek human help and direction, but when it is not there, he knows our need. He loves us and will guide us himself. Even when we do have human help, it is the Holy Spirit who is our real director. Paul of the Cross constantly refers to the Holy Spirit as the one who guides and directs, especially in prayer. The human director is a help to catch the voice and love-indications the Holy Spirit gives us.

A Holy Director Helps

Paul urged Sister Colomba Gandolfi to pray for a good director. "You need a learned and holy director, so ask this of God in prayer" (II, 500). He tells her this in more than one letter and gives this reason,

"Ask the grace from the Lord that he would provide a holy director so that you can walk with more liberty of spirit without fear" (II,497). It does help to have human reassurance as to the way in which we are walking, especially since the Way, which is Jesus, is not the way most people walk. When we walk this way we are bound to meet with much misunderstanding and even opposition. A good director is an invaluable help at such times.

Discerning the Spirit

We also need help in discerning the voice of the Holy Spirit and not confusing it with our own feelings. In Chapter 5 we considered the difference between faith and feelings. A good director can help us sort them out. Paul writes to Agnes Grazi, "Do not believe in your heart, in your feelings, and especially in any interior voices, all the more so when they are not of things for the great glory of God. For the most part they are from your own spirit or from the devil" (I, 147). Paul uses heart here as synonymous with feelings and not as elsewhere for our will, our power of choice, deeper within us than our feelings. If we do not have help, it is easy to mistake our own feelings for the voice of God. Here is where a director can be of great assistance.

It is so difficult to tell the practical difference between our feelings and our faith. We start out life letting our feelings be our guide in everything. If we like something (liking, or pleasure, is a feeling), we do it or at least try to do it. If we don't like it or perhaps are afraid of it (fear is a feeling), we avoid it as far as possible. This manner of acting becomes instinctive in us and we don't even realize that this is what is happening. When we want to follow Jesus and let the voice of His Holy Spirit be our guide, it is hard to hear that voice when we are so accustomed to listen to the voices of our feelings.

Faith is Unfelt

We are very much aware of our feelings and much less aware of our faith. This lack of awareness makes it all the more difficult to believe that the Spirit is really guiding us. Our faith, through which we hear and follow the voice of the Spirit, is something unfelt, which we have to learn to hear and discern deep inside of us. For this we ordinarily need help and Paul was constantly assisting those he directed in this way. Such discernment, in Paul's opinion, was one of the important functions of a spiritual director.

One of the difficulties in this is that for one who is striving to follow Jesus closely, feelings can often be religious feelings. They are often called consolations and frequently come during prayer or some religious experience, such as a retreat, cursillo, charismatic prayer meeting, or even when alone. It is common for beginners in the life of prayer to have many such pleasant feelings of God, or consolations. The experience of Peter, James and John at the Transfiguration is an example. But as the Spirit leads a person deeper into the Christian life, these consolations usually fade away and what is left is the darkness of faith, which is unfelt. This can be very distressing and confusing. Here is where a good director is so important to reassure a person that he or she is on the right path and is not going backwards because feelings are not there any more.

Furthermore, it is necessary to positively let go of these feelings so as not to hinder growth in the spirit. Here is the way Paul put it to a Sister he was directing, "Anyone walking in a garden looks rather at the fruits and flowers than at the leaves. The leaves are the consolations which we should neither notice nor desire. The flowers are the holy desires, and yearnings to suffer great things for the Supreme Good and his honor and glory. The fruits, which are more precious and dear to Jesus Crucified are the virtues we need" (IV, 101).

This analogy of Paul is a beautiful one, but we have to be aware, not only of the points of comparison, but also the points of difference, as we do with every analogy. All analogies have their limitations, even the parables of Jesus. The fruits are the most desirable products of the tree and the virtues are the most desirable products of a life under the influence of the Holy Spirit. However, the leaves have their purpose too, though Paul was not using their particular purpose in his analogy. Feelings have their purpose too, though Paul does not go into that. They are meant to encourage us, especially in the beginning, but they are not the goal of the interior life, nor are they the standard for judging progress.

The virtues are the fruits, but here is where the analogy does not apply. We can see and taste fruits on a tree, but we cannot see and taste our virtues. We have to trust that they are there when we are following the lead of the Holy Spirit as we hear him. When we give our lives to the Lord, we have to trust that he is leading and guiding us, even though we cannot feel that we are making progress. We have to let the leaves on the tree, the feelings, go, and simply trust God that the fruit is growing as it should. If we were not, he would let us know, not through our feelings, hut through our awareness that we were deliberately refusing something he was asking of us. We need to come to the peace we spoke of in the last chapter, the peace of not even looking for signs, but just going forward, trusting that if we were not following the Spirit, God would let us know by unmistakable signs.

Those who are not as open to the Lord as they should be do not like to admit, even to themselves that they may be deliberately refusing God something. These people usually turn to the tactic of not listening to him. They are afraid of what he might ask them and so they prefer not to listen, often under the pretext that God doesn't speak to them anyway. However, if we are refusing to listen, especially because of fear of what God might ask of us, we know it deep down. As long as we are willing to listen and follow where he leads, then we are on the right road, even though we feel nothing, even though we might feel that our faults are increasing, even though we might feel that God is displeased with us or has left us.

Fear of Deception

A temptation that often comes up in this regard is to wonder, "Maybe God is speaking to me and I am just not hearing him." If a mother looked out her kitchen window and saw her little child starting to cross a busy street in disobedience to her orders, would she just whisper in his direction or speak so softly that he could not hear her? She would make certain that the child heard her voice telling him not to cross that street. Is God less concerned for his children if they should start to head the wrong way? He does not speak in "maybes" where the direction of his children is concerned. Paul had to keep reassuring those he directed that they were on the right road when they were afraid of being deceived because they no longer had the feelings they did in the beginning of their walk with God.

Paul believed too that a good director was a help in avoiding deception. He writes to one Sister, "Be sincere with whomever is directing your spirit and manifest to him the graces God gives you and their effects in you, as also your failures. You need a learned and experienced director so that you won't be deceived and will walk a straight path on the road of perfection and sanctity" (IV, 101). To a married woman he writes, "Confess your faults as you see them, but do not be disturbed over them" (I, 61). It is a common temptation to want to look good in the eyes of the one directing us and to omit mentioning any defects that we are afraid might bring us down in his or her opinion. For good direction, as Paul saw it, absolute honesty was needed.

Pride Interferes

The defect we all have that can make this honesty difficult and even painful is pride. That is why Paul could say that humility is so necessary to accept direction and to be open with the director. Strangely enough, though, humility is needed not only to be willing to look bad before the director but even in looking good and receiving commendation from him or her. Paul writes to Sister Colomba Gandolfi, "You have sincerely disclosed to me all your defects and temptations. His divine Majesty has made it clear to me that this work in you is entirely his. Nothing remains but to praise the divine Goodness and to be grateful to our good God" (II, 457).

Probably the reason why we hesitate to declare even our virtues and qualities is that we don't want to look proud. Paul's approach in this matter was the same as a saint he admired so much, Teresa of Avila. She tells us that it is not humility to deny the gifts of God, but ingratitude. However, we need to recognize them as his gifts, not just as our own accomplishments.

Direction is Personal

Paul gives other practical tidbits for those receiving spiritual direction. Sometimes those who have a good spiritual director are apt to try to direct others with the direction they have received, or at least to share their direction with others. Paul did not think this was a good idea since the same direction does not fit all. He writes to Thomas Fossi, "The counsels given for your own interior should not serve as a rule to have others walk the same way. God deals with one in one way, another in another" (I, 581). The more personal any direction is, the less it should be shared. General principles are usually safe to share, hut particular recommendations given to one may not fit others.

For example, a spiritual director might advise a married woman to yield to her husband in a matter that was more or less indifferent, but which was not her preferred way of doing things. If she were to share this advice with another woman whose need was to stand up and confront her husband in a matter of importance, the advice would be harmful.

Perseverance Under Direction

Another recommendation of Paul was not to leave direction because of difficulties or trials. He writes to Sister Cherubina Bresciani that her idea of leaving direction was a temptation of the devil. "Don't be surprised that the devil when he is angry tries to distract you with suggestions that you should leave spiritual direction" (I, 439). It is a common temptation not to want to talk to a director in time of upsetness and confusion. The temptation is to wait till we have it "all together." But this is precisely when we need direction the most. It is much harder to talk and share when we are upset and confused and don't know how to present things, or even where to begin. Yet this is usually the best time. If we wait till everything seems clear, the clarity may be only apparent and not from the Lord.

Discernment of Direction Itself

Paul also has much to say that is helpful to directors. For one thing, he did not believe that a director should accept someone for guidance until God gave clear signs that he should do this. He wrote to Agnes Grazi that he himself had acted this way in her regard and had discerned it carefully before he agreed to direct her (I, 154). He believed that spiritual direction was a serious responsibility and should not be undertaken rashly.

Once he had God's signs, though, that he was to direct a certain person, Paul trusted that God would give him all he needed for that function. He writes to Agnes, "If God should want me to be of help to others, he would give me all that would be necessary, especially for the direction of souls" (I, 303). Naturally Paul believed that God would do the same for all spiritual directors, once they had discerned that God wanted them to engage in the direction of this or that particular person.

Paul has very high standards for spiritual directors. He expresses it this way, "A director ought to be a very learned man, a great man of prayer and a man of wide experience" (I, 178). He adds another practical consideration when writing to Thomas Fossi concerning the director Thomas should have. He should be "a holy, learned and prudent man of much experience who can give recommendations which are according to God and *if only* he were nearby that would be a great advantage" (I, 723). Paul said this because Thomas wanted

Paul to he his director and the distance between them was probably a two or three day's journey. These days, of course, it is possible to find someone who can be a good director even at a distance since modern travel shrinks distance. If visits to a director do not have to be too frequent, it is possible to travel great distances to find a director who has the qualities Paul speaks of. Paul did not care for direction by letter, even though by force of necessity he had to do so much of it that way. He wrote to one lady who wanted him to direct her, "I have no way of giving you direction, since I am too far away and I don't know anything of your spirit either in writing or in person" (I, 380). However, we can thank God he did do so much direction by letter, since we have the fruits of his wisdom today through the letters that he wrote.

Paul believed that a director should be detached from those he directed, while at the same time a great love bond could grow up between a director and those God entrusts to him. (See Chapter 1: "Love For Those He Directed.") Paul also believed that it was necessary to be detached from direction itself, which he called a "most noble, but most fatiguing and dangerous occupation" (I, 176). He believed that a director should always leave those he directed free to seek out someone else for direction. He left Agnes Grazi and others he directed free to consult with any other confessor or director they wished (I, 130). A director should not be possessive.

There is no such thing as a perfect spiritual director. But if a person is called to direction of another by God, then that person can count on God's grace to be able to give appropriate direction, and to grow in holiness by the very occupation.

CHAPTER 15

Mystical Death

We now come to one of Paul's favorite ideas which he tried to share with those he directed, the idea of mystical death. Even the words themselves can be scary as Paul himself admits. However, the concept goes back to our root tradition beginning with Jesus himself. To use one of his own expressions, "If the grain of wheat that falls to the ground does not die, it remains just a grain of wheat, but if it dies it bears much fruit" (Jn 12:24). But what does this mean? To what do we die?

Sometimes the expression refers to bodily death itself, as it did to Jesus, and also to those who have imitated Jesus in accepting physical death when their faith required it. These we call martyrs. But most are called to die in other ways. Paul the apostle speaks of dying to sin, "You, too, must consider yourselves as dead to sin" (Rm 6:11). The Epistle to the Colossians is somewhat more specific. "Put to death those parts of you which are earthly: fornication, impurity, passion, evil desires, and that greed which is idolatry" (3:5). This admonition refers to those who have just become Christians and are struggling with the grosser forms of sin. However, the principle applies to other forms of death. Let us look at some of the things Paul of the Cross has to say about this matter.

The Fullness of Detachment

For Paul, mystical death was the fullness of detachment. He writes to Lucy Burlini, "I beseech you as far as possible to obey the gentle interior invitations of the Holy Spirit. Jesus wills from you a *complete detachment* from all that is created, *a true mystical death* [Italics mine] to all that is not God, a great nudity and poverty of spirit, to be entirely clothed in the most pure faith and holy love of Jesus Christ. Oh, Lucy, listen to the most sweet voice of your heavenly Spouse!" (II, 717). One of the ways Paul counteracts the fearsomeness of the expression is to connect it with Jesus' love, as he instinctively does on most occasions.

Writing to Agnes Grazi, Paul is even more detailed and expresses his excitement. "Surrender yourself more and more to God with great detachment from all creatures and complete self-annihilation; you will experience great results and I hope shall be inflamed with love. Oh, my child in Jesus Christ, when, oh when shall we be dead to everything to live only for our God? When, oh when? Oh, precious death, more longed for than life, death which makes us divine because we are all transformed in God by love! Come now, let us look forward to this death to all created things. But to die, my child, you have to suffer great pain. Who can ever describe the pains suffered by those who endure the death of the body? Suffice it to say, they are so many and so great that they sever the soul from the body.

"Something like this, one might say, happens to servants of God who die to all consolation. Oh, what distress must be suffered, what affliction from within and from without, what interior and exterior conflicts! What aridity and depression! What darkness of mind! What fear of deception! What anxiety over being abandoned, for it seems to the soul that it has lost God! All these, my child, are so many ways and means of dying to creatures to live only to God and for God" (I, 180).

Death to Creatures

What does Paul (and other mystics like him) mean by dying to all creatures, all that is not God, all that is created. (The expression, "all that is not God," Paul found in John Tauler, whom, as we have seen previously, Paul loved and used so much.) Are we not supposed to love everyone as Jesus has taught us? How can we be detached from those we love? And are we not supposed to love the world God has made, and take good care of it so that it will serve the needs of all?

Mystical language tries to describe what is actually being experienced and does not always qualify things sufficiently for general understanding. Those who have similar experiences understand it. Those who have not had at least some experience similar to that of the mystics often fail to understand their language. Paul does say something else to Agnes, though, which gives us a clue to the answers we would like for our questions. He writes, "I am happy that God is depriving you of all contentment to learn to serve God with greater purity of intention. Oh, how good it is to remain on the cross with Jesus, without seeing him and without enjoying him. This is the short way to reach that happy death to all that is created, to live more purely in the uncreated and immense Good. On such occasions, when the soul finds itself stripped in this way, there is nothing else to do than gently express your faith in the divine Presence, and to remain lost in God, abandoning yourself into that immense sea of love, without looking for your own enjoyment but for the divine good pleasure" (I, 139-140).

Death to Self-Satisfaction

Now Paul speaks a little more precisely. It is not so much creatures from whom we are to be detached or other people (whom we are to love dearly in Christ), but our own satisfaction from them. Death and detachment are really not from others, even though it is often expressed that way, but from ourselves and our own instinctive self-seeking.

If we would connect this with what Scripture has said about death to sin, we might remember that we are all born in sin. To use a modern expression, we are all faultily programmed. We are instinctively selfish and not instinctively loving. We enjoy *receiving* love, but we do not naturally enjoy *giving* it. One time a small boy was expressing his pleasure to me that Christmas was coming in just a few more days. I said to him, "Isn't that great? What are you going to give this Christmas?" He was speechless. Obviously, his idea of Christmas was *getting* rather than *giving*.

We all have something in us of that preference for getting instead of giving, even though we may have given our lives to Jesus and want to do nothing but please him in everything. We want to give by the power of free choice or free will. But we do not want to by natural inclination when the loving thing is something we naturally find difficult or even repugnant to do. The Spirit is at work to heal us so that we can easily respond to the demands of love, no matter how difficult they may be. Of course, this is a process that takes a lifetime to complete and may not even seem complete at death. But the Spirit is working at this inner transformation at all times. For this to take place we must be willing to die to the natural satisfactions we all seek. We do not plan or direct this process; God does. Paul encourages those he directs to be willing to accept the detachment from self-seeking that the Spirit is bringing about in them.

God Detaches Us

This total death to self and complete detachment is not something we can accomplish ourselves but something that God has to do in us. Paul writes, "Attend to a total abandonment to the divine good pleasure and a true detachment from all that is created.... From this you will build a great palace of perfection, or, to put it in a better way, God will build it in you with your cooperation, and there he will take his delight" (II, 5).

Naturally, Paul does not use the expression "reprogramming," but he does express the same thing in other ways. He writes to Agnes, "Aridity is a hidden treasure and God works through it to deprive you of all contentment, so that God alone might become the contentment of your contentment" (I, 107). God wants us to be happy. But he knows that happiness does not come from satisfying our feelings, whether in things or other people, or even in prayer and in the things of God. So He strips us or reprograms us to the extent that we let him, so that we might discover a deeper form of joy which is not on the feeling level — joy in God and in giving ourselves to him with no felt return. It is something like what St. Thérèse, the Little Flower, expressed when she said, "I want a love that is not felt."

Willingness to Suffer

To reach such inner peace and joy we must be willing to experience this death. Using the words of Jesus about the grain of wheat dying Paul says, "The soul is a grain which God sows in the great field which is the Church, and to bear fruit, it must die in sufferings, contradictions, sorrows, persecutions, and so forth. When it is dead to all, in the midst of these pains, it bears abundant fruit" (I, 335). The fruits he refers to are chiefly the virtues, as we have seen before. These virtues include love of others. So we die to the self-satisfaction we might find in others to love them with a love that is pure and free of all self-seeking.

Detachment and Love

For example, Paul loved Agnes Grazi very dearly and she loved him. But he did not want any attachment in this love in either direction. He writes to her, "There are those who believe that you are attached to me, but I know that this is not true. At every moment we have to fear the fierce beast of self-love which is a dragon with seven heads who interferes in everything" (I, 222). In other words, Paul is really equating detachment from others with detachment from self, or self-love. Naturally he is not speaking of that normal love and healthy self-esteem that God expects of us. Writers of Paul's time were much more apt to speak of the dangers of inordinate love of self than to speak of that healthy love of self Jesus refers to in citing the commandment to love our neighbor as ourselves (Mt 19:19). Paul is speaking rather of that love of self which puts self-satisfaction above God's will and the real good of others. It is this type of self-love to which we need to die and from which we need to be detached. When Paul and other mystics speak of dying to self and to all other creatures, this is what they mean. Perhaps the language used is not the most understandable in our times, but they are speaking about profound spiritual truths which are most difficult to express no matter what human language is used.

Paul does make some attempt at distinguishing for Agnes the difference between loving others and being attached when he says, "Love everyone in God, but don't be attached to anyone" (I, 110). The detachment Paul speaks of is not the same as coldness, or aloofness, or separation. Loving in a detached way means loving without seeking one's own satisfaction in the love, but rather the good of the one who is loved. We can be most sure we are loving in this way when we reach out to someone to whom we are not naturally attracted. That is why God has to send people of this type into our lives so that we can gradually learn to love everyone (even those we naturally like) with a love that is free of self-seeking. It is easy to reach out to those we like, thinking we are loving with a divine love, when all we are doing is following our natural attractions. But in the case of those we don't naturally like, we can be sure it is divine love when we reach out to them when it is needed. The same is true of those we do like ordinarily, but not when they are doing something displeasing to us. Providence arranges situations like this to give us an opportunity to grow in selfless love.

Jesus puts it this way: "If you love those who love you, what credit is that to you?" (Lk 6:32). We naturally reach out to those who are attractive to us and give us some natural satisfaction. But to reach out to those who do not is something more than our weak human nature can do without the grace of the Holy Spirit. On the other hand, we need to reach out to those we like, not for the satisfaction we get in them, but for their own sake. This is where death and detachment come in. The Holy Spirit has to detach us from dependence on this self-satisfaction in others so that we will love with a love that is sheer giving, as Jesus loves, and not with a hook that seeks something back for self. This is true mystical death.

Need to Receive

This does not mean that we always give and never receive. We need to receive, to be loved. But we don't have to maneuver or manipulate others to get this love. We have to trust that God knows our love-needs and will move others to love us freely. He might not always give it through the ones from whom we would prefer to receive it, but the love will come from somewhere, sometimes from most unexpected sources. We need to be able to receive love that is freely given by others and, instead of trying to force it from one particular individual, we have to let it come from whomever.

Here is an example of a natural human tendency to manipulate love from others instead of waiting till it comes freely. Suppose a man comes home from work irritated because his boss has piled more work on him than he thinks he should have. He comes home to a wife who is upset because their clumsy son has just knocked over their best lamp. If she starts to talk first, he is going to have to fight himself and call on all his detachment from self-seeking to listen to her till she finishes and not interrupt her to talk about his own problem. The same would be true on her part if he started first. In order to love with a truly Christ like love, each one would have to die to self to reach out to the other.

Certainly there are heavier crosses than extra work or broken articles in the home. Paul writes to Agnes Grazi's sister-in-law, Mary Jane Venturi Grazi concerning the terminal illness of her husband, "I know you do not stop and will not stop praying to the Lord to grant him to end his life with a holy death" (II,42). Here there is a very painful detachment and death to self required. Detachment from heavy crosses like this is prepared for by detachment from little ones all along, like the broken articles in the house. As Jesus has said, "Whoever is faithful in very little, is also faithful in much" (Lk 16:10).

This is a key point for Paul. God is in charge of everything. As Scripture puts it, "God accomplishes all things in accordance with the purpose he has decided upon" (Ep 1:11). Many people become discouraged when they hear or read about this or that requirement for reaching the fullness of divine life. This discouragement often comes from the presumption that progress is something they have to bring about themselves, as if God had given them a big do-it-yourself kit and then went about his business leaving the rest up to them, only helping from time to time if they got stuck. These people usually presume that if God were directing everything, it would destroy our free will.

Free will is a clear teaching of Sacred Scripture and of our Christian faith. So is God's universal and constant causality. How these two teachings go together is a mystery that has baffled theologians for centuries and probably will continue to baffle them till the end of time, as we have already considered in Chapter 2. We have to learn to become comfortable with mystery: to accept seemingly contradictory teachings of faith without being able to understand how they fit together. Human free will and God's universal causality are two such teachings. Yet the saints and mystics never seemed to have a problem with mystery. They could accept God as doing all things and yet themselves as being free. Paul certainly accepted both facets of this mystery.

CHAPTER 16

Death and Detachment

After looking at Paul's idea of mystical death and seeing the connection he makes between this death and detachment, let us look at other aspects of the detachment God has to bring about in us that can be puzzling. Here is a first example. One of the things Paul speaks of as something we need to be detached from is something that seems to be nothing but good: namely the gifts of God. He writes to Sister Columba Gandolfi, "I recommend to you not to remain in the enjoyment of spirit that the gifts of God produce, but with a gentle glance of faith and love, take your interior flight into God more each time in nudity and poverty of spirit. Lose everything in him, without looking either for joy or suffering, not at insights and understandings of spirit, but resting purely in naked faith and pure love in the bosom of God, entirely clothed with Jesus crucified" (II, 462).

God does give gifts and we need to be grateful for them. However, it is easy to use the gifts of God for selfish purposes. Examples would be: thinking over some gift of God, not with the idea of thanking him for it, but with the secret purpose of puffing up our own pride; or sharing some gift with others with the secret desire that they will esteem us more highly as a spiritual person. Paul asked those he directed to die to any satisfaction to self in God's gifts; simply to use them for his honor and glory and to seek God himself, not just the gifts.

We need to die, not only to our own enjoyment, but even to our own understanding. Paul writes to Agnes, "Oh, my daughter! Fortunate is that soul which is detached from its own understanding! This is a most profound lesson. God will enable you to learn it if you put all your contentment in the cross of Jesus Christ, in dying to all that is not God on the cross of the Savior" (I, 107).

It is only natural to want to understand things and to judge things by the criterion of our own understanding. For example, if a mother of three small children dies of cancer at 35, we could easily say, "Why does something like this happen? How could God love her or those children if he lets this happen to them?" When Jesus wept at the death of Lazarus, there were those who asked, "How could he let Lazarus die if he loved him?" (Jn 11:35-37). The question is a natural one. We can feel with someone who would ask a question like this and share their pain with them. But there is no intellectual answer possible. Paul would have those he directed understand this impossibility and die even to their own desires to find an intellectual answer.

Exactly how Paul would handle questions about a premature death is hard to say. Certainly he would advise not looking for an intellectual solution to something that is in the realm of mystery. But the question of how could God love us when he does things like that, Paul would not even consider a valid question. For Paul, God's love was a given that could never be questioned. Paul believed that God has already given us ample evidence that he loves us totally and completely and that everything he does comes from love and leads to love. No matter what happens, his love is unquestionable. Whatever the answer to the "why" question, there could never be even the faintest possibility that God was not doing something loving. Neither would Paul ever suggest that God is not really the one doing it and that every unpleasant event has faulty human beings or perhaps uncontrollable natural forces behind it. For Paul, God was God, all-powerful, all-knowing and totally in control of everything. However, he also believed what his namesake, Paul the apostle had said long before, "Now we know that the Spirit works in every way for the good of those who love God and are called in accordance with his plan" (Rm 8:28). When we accept God's love and total control in faith, then there are bound to be some things that God does that are beyond our understanding. At such times we have to die to our desire to understand and simply trust in God's goodness and love. In this mortal life, we are just not capable of understanding all that God does.

Paul writes to a nun, "Don't be curious to want to understand all the divine workings" (III, 66). It is so hard not to be curious and to leave things we can't understand in God's loving hands. That is why Paul says to the same Sister, "Be detached and support yourself completely on the will of God." We need support because things that are puzzling to us are often very painful as well. Here is where we need that support that comes from God, of which Jesus speaks when he says,

"Come to me all you who labor and are heavy burdened and I will give you rest" (Mt 11:28). However, we can save ourselves a lot of interior pain if we do not even try to understand these things, but simply trust the love of God to bring them to good for us. If they are things that happen to others, we need to feel with them, as Scripture says, "Bear one another's burdens, and in this way you will fulfill Christ's law" (Gal 6:2). We need to help one another as we struggle together to walk in the footsteps of Jesus crucified.

God Detaches Us

Certainly we do not know all the things from which we need to be detached and to which we need to die. God does, though, and he arranges circumstances to bring this detachment about. He asks us to be willing to accept what he is doing. However, this willingness is often on the level of intention and free will and not on the level of feeling. Paul goes into this aspect of the mystery in writing to one of his own Passionist religious, "Examine yourself to see if your intention is most pure. Every day seek to render that intention deiform, that is, entirely divine, performing all your actions in God and for his love alone, uniting your work with that of Jesus Christ, our Lord, who is our Way, Truth and Life [Jn 14:6]. Most beloved sons! 'You are dead and your life is hidden with Christ in God" [Col 3:3]. Therefore, as dead to all that is not God, keep yourself completely detached from all that is created in total poverty and nudity of spirit, with great detachment from all sensible consolations" (IV, 226).

Detachment from Feelings

When Paul, and theologians generally, speak of sensible consolations, they mean feelings: enjoyable feelings that often come in prayer, after retreats or other spiritual experiences, such as charismatic prayer meetings, cursillos, marriage encounters, and so forth. Paul is saying we need to be detached from the pleasure we get from these feelings.

Feelings like these are gifts from God, but they are like candy given to a child. Candy is usually given to make life a little easier for the child. The child needs to learn to face more and more difficult things in life in order to mature. Parents who understand this give a child less and less candy and the sweet things of life, which are often escapes from facing challenges. God does the same with us. He gradually takes away the sweetness of consolations and gives us fewer and fewer pleasant spiritual feelings that we may mature and be able to face more and more difficult things in our inner process of growth. Unless we have help to understand this process, we are apt to take the lessening of feelings as a bad sign. It may seem that we are going backwards. So often we hear good people say, "I used to feel so good when I prayed. Now I don't get any feelings at all. What has gone wrong?" Nothing has gone wrong. As Paul and other spiritual writers, especially St. John of the Cross, often say, feelings are not our guide on this journey: faith is. Faith is our surrender to God, dark and without feelings.

Agnes Grazi experienced this loss of feelings as she drew closer to God, and she too was afraid something was going wrong. She wrote to Paul about this and he answered her, "God wants you to be deprived of all your human consolations. He wants your heart to have no other comfort except that which God gives.... Therefore my daughter in Jesus Christ, let your fears cease. God is your guide and your Father, master and spouse. Abandon yourself into the divine bosom of his most holy good pleasure" (I, 209).

Trust God's Leadings

It is hard for most of us to be convinced that we are making progress when we don't feel it. It is a natural tendency to try to recapture those experiences and situations in which we used to feel so good spiritually. But in order to make progress, we need to let go of any striving after spiritual feelings and simply trust God that he is watching us at every moment, leading us and loving us. He will always let us know if we are on the wrong road, but is usually silent when we are on the right road. We remarked previously that there are signs on exits of freeways that say WRONG WAY, but none that say RIGHT WAY. When we are on the right way to God, we don't need signs either.

Some people say, "Maybe God is speaking to me and I just don't hear him." God loves us too much to leave us in doubt. If he says something to us and we don't hear him, he speaks again, louder each time. He does not speak in "maybes." The only ones who do not hear him are those who do not want to listen, perhaps for fear of what he might say. Those who are open to anything the Lord wants of them will understand both his voice and his silence. Those who are not open to the Lord know it deep down, even though they might pretend to be hearing him and possibly convince themselves that they are hearing him.

Others might say, "I thought I was listening to the Lord, but what I decided to do after much prayer turned out to be a mistake." Mistakes do not mean that a person was not listening. God does not prevent all human mistakes but uses them for our growth.

Signs of Progress

It is helpful to be aware of what are good signs of progress and what are not in the interior life. When there are fewer and fewer great feelings in prayer or in any other spiritual activity, it is not a bad sign, but a good one. We need to walk in the darkness of faith, knowing that we want to please God and trusting that he is doing something wonderful in the depths of our being. God's silence is a good sign. If we were on the wrong road, he would not be silent. Paul of the Cross, John of the Cross, and all masters of the spiritual life emphasize this.

However, as we go along, we may become more and more aware of our negative feelings, and think that surely they must be a bad sign. We may find more repugnance for the things of God, more reluctance for the detachment and death required as the Holy Spirit strips us of more and more of our attachments. We don't usually notice how attached we are until the Holy Spirit starts stripping from us our attachments to pleasures and comforts, agreeable situations and the desire to relate only to people with whom we are comfortable. Yet even all these negative feelings are not a bad sign. They are triggered off by the increasing weight of the crosses the Lord has to ask us to carry. Usually we don't notice that our crosses are getting heavier, just that we are finding more repugnance for the things of God and find it hard to be convinced that we are not going backwards.

It is important not to take feelings as a bad sign one way or the other. As Paul writes to his own religious, it is the "intention" that is important. God looks at our intentions. Paul does not use this word as some do when they say that hell is paved with good intentions. By "intentions" they mean halfhearted desires. Paul means by this word firm and definite choices to do something God wants of us. God looks at our intentions, which are firm, not at our feelings over which we often have little or no control.

We certainly cannot always feel an attraction to the sufferings needed for our purification and growth. Jesus did not feel an attraction for his Passion in Gethsemane. But his intention was to choose his Father's will. He expressed his agonized feelings to his Father, knowing that the Father understood the difference between his will, his free choice, and the feelings that were only natural under the circumstances. The same thing is bound to happen to us, though in a far lesser degree as we follow in the footsteps of Jesus. We will find that mystical death often involves a death to feelings, that is, death to relying on them and taking them as standards. We need to know that feelings about the things of God, no matter how unpleasant they may be, are not a sign that faith is being either lost or lessened. They are only a sign that we are as human as Jesus.

Dying with Jesus

In his little Treatise on Mystical Death Paul speaks of the thousand deaths we have to undergo before dying and of the fears we have of these deaths. But for him, the fear was eased when he considered this death as the response to a desire of Jesus that we should die with him on the cross.

It was a big help to Paul to see his own sufferings in the light of the Passion. He puts it this way, "I will try with all my strength to follow the footsteps of Jesus. If I am afflicted, abandoned, desolate, I will keep him company in the Garden. If I am despised and injured, I will keep him company in the Praetorium. If I am depressed and afflicted in the agonies of suffering, I will keep him company faithfully on the Mount, and in a generous spirit I will keep him company on the Cross with the lance in my heart. Oh, how sweet it is to die! (Treatise on Mystical Death, IV)."

We could add to this litany, "If I have lies told about me, I will keep him company in the courtroom. If I am treated unfairly and unjustly, I will keep him company before Pilate. If my friends leave me and disown me, I will keep him company as He looked at Peter in the courtyard." We could go on and on and find some connection with just about any aspect of the Passion and whatever we have to go through. The important thing is not just to think about Jesus and how he might have felt in these phases of his Passion, but to adopt his attitude, his intention, towards all these situations. Jesus chose these sufferings as drops in the cup the Father was giving him. He did this in all trust that the Father would bring good out of the situation in some way, even after his death. Jesus had to die to his own feelings and natural preferences, and through his Passion, we can receive the grace to do the same.

Paul makes this connection between the deaths found in the Passion and their positive effects in a letter to Lucy Burlini, "Jesus wants of you a most profound detachment from all that is created, a true mystical death to all that is not God, great nudity and poverty of spirit, to be entirely clothed with the most pure faith and holy love of Jesus Christ. Oh, Lucy, listen to the most sweet voice of your heavenly Spouse" (II, 717).

The thought of dying to anything is not naturally a pleasant thought. Death has a certain ring of finality to it, especially when it is death to something we naturally enjoy. We need to remember that for Paul (and for the whole Christian tradition) death was only a stage in the process that leads to a transforming resurrection, as Jesus has shown by going before us. For this reason, we need to focus more on what comes after the death, whatever the particular death may be. Paul speaks of the positive results that come after this mystical death.

Writing to Agnes, he says, "Oh, my daughter, God wants great things! He calls you to the highest perfection. To arrive at this, your cooperation is needed. You must annihilate yourself before God in a spirit of true and most simple humility, with a great detachment from all that is created, and from your own life, with a total transformation into the divine good pleasure and a total abandonment into that abyss of infinite goodness" (I, 132).

These beautiful words of Paul sum up what he meant by mystical death and detachment. But this only leads to something further as we will consider in the next chapter.

——

CHAPTER 17

Mystical Nativity and Spiritual Childhood

*P*aul never speaks of mystical death as an end, but as the beginning of something new. It is only human to think of death as an end, since we have not actually experienced what goes on after death. We know it only in faith, and much depends on how strong or how insightful our faith is. But for Paul, mystical death was the beginning of a new life, which he often speaks of as mystical nativity. He writes to Mother Mary Crucified, "On the coming Solemnity of Christmas, I will not fail to ask the sovereign divine Infant to renew in your spirit at every moment that mystical divine nativity, so that your spirit may be reborn at every moment to a life that is divine and holy. This sacred mystical divine nativity is celebrated every day in the deepest interior solitude. In this sacred desert, in profound separation and detachment from every created thing, in total nudity and poverty of spirit, and in a sacred silence of faith and love, the human soul is reborn in the divine-humanized Word to a new life that is entirely holy and divine" (II, 310).

In human life, birth comes before death, but in the inner life of the spirit, it is just the opposite: mystical death comes before mystical nativity. In the last chapter we saw that Paul wished that Thomas Fossi would experience mystical death so that he might experience mystical nativity. The paradox of death before life is seen in the death and resurrection of Jesus. The Fathers of the Church often called the resurrection his second birth, his birth to a new and risen life. Even the anniversaries of the deaths of the martyrs were called their "birthdays."

Connected in Paul's mind with the idea of mystical nativity was another related concept, the idea of "spiritual childhood," a mystery and a truth that was to be developed so beautifully in the next century by St. Thérèse of Lisieux. Paul writes to Agnes, "Let yourself be broken and reduced to nothing and live abandoned on the loving bosom of God as a baby. Let yourself be guided by him" (I, 221). He writes to Sister Cherubina Bresciani, "You will please God all the more as you are more resigned to his divine will, and when you remain as a simple baby, reposing on the loving bosom of Jesus Christ, there letting die mystically all your cares, desires and inclinations, even good ones, remaining in true interior solitude with true humility of heart and perfect abandonment to the divine good pleasure" (I, 506).

Docility and Freedom from Care

In these statements, Paul considers two characteristics of babies: one of which is docility, letting itself be carried everywhere by the mother; the other is freedom from care, since the baby expects that the mother will take care of everything. Paul would have those he directed become as docile as little children to the guidance of the Holy Spirit and utterly peaceful, knowing that divine Providence is taking care of everything. Even these characteristics, though, are not something we can acquire by our own efforts, but something the Spirit has to do in us as we allow him to work. Notice too that Paul connects mystical death with becoming children, two ideas that we don't usually put together.

Childlike Confidence

There is another characteristic of babies which Paul mentions in a letter to Thomas Fossi, "Take from the Lord what he gives you, like a baby which accepts whatever the mother gives it" (I, 78). We need such confidence in God that we believe he will give us all we need if we trust him, ask him, and simply open our hands to receive it. We need to trust too, as a baby does, that even if we are unable to ask or don't know what to ask for, he will give it to us anyway when he sees that we need it, as would a good and attentive mother.

Spiritual Childhood and the Passion

Paul connects this spiritual childhood with the Passion of Jesus. He writes to Agnes, "If the sweet Baby draws you to his little house, go there.... Read in the mirror of the divine Infant, read, I say, how to become poor, little, dead, crucified, and buried to all" (I, 97). Paul considered that Jesus never lost his childlike spirit, not even on the cross. In a certain manner of speaking we might say that the child Jesus was crucified for us.

We need to be childlike to understand the Passion. Paul writes, "This secret (of solitude) is learned at the foot of the Crucified, since it is revealed only to little ones and is hidden from the learned and clever of this world" [Mt 11:25] (III, 90). The learned and the clever cannot understand Christ crucified in their wisdom, as Paul the apostle writes (1 Cor 1:21-25). They look for human reasons behind the Passion and cannot find any, so they reject it as foolish. But a childlike spirit catches the message of love and doesn't look for any other reasons. The same thing is true of trying to understand our own sufferings which continue the Passion. The fact that they do continue it is expressed beautifully in words attributed to Paul the apostle, "I rejoice in what I'm suffering for you now; in my flesh I'm completing what is lacking in Christ's afflictions on behalf of his body, that is, the church" (Col 1:24). Human reason cannot figure out the reason for our sufferings, but a childlike acceptance of God's love is satisfied not to have reasons as long as we know his all-powerful love is behind them.

It takes a childlike attitude to come to that wisdom Paul the apostle speaks of in his letter to the Corinthians mentioned above. Paul of the Cross expresses a similar insight when he says, "God is pleased with those who make themselves little and become as little children. These he holds on his divine breast and nourishes them with the milk and most sweet wine of holy love. This inebriates those who drink it, but this is a holy drunkenness which makes one grow constantly in wisdom" (I, 308).

Here Paul speaks of the deep and simple wisdom to which a childlike spirit opens us, a wisdom taught by the Holy Spirit, as Paul the apostle says (1 Cor 2:10-13). In the image of drunkenness which Paul of the Cross connects with it, he alludes to that joyful and playful spirit of children which saints often exhibit to a surprising degree. This childlike spirit is something which Jesus possessed all his life, as we have said. He kept it also in his risen life..

Spiritual Childhood and the Resurrection

If it was the child Jesus who was crucified for us, it was also in a way the child Jesus who rose for us, since the mystery of spiritual childhood is continued even in his resurrection. Paul considered the resurrection of Jesus, as did the Fathers of the Church, a new birth; not merely a second birth of the same kind as the first, but a birth to something new.

In considering the death and resurrection of Jesus, many people think of the resurrection as a return to life. It is less a return, however, than a passing on, a Passover, as it was called by the early Christians, to a new and divine life. Resurrection does not merely mean taking up again our former life, but of being transformed to a new life of total love. We are used to thinking of it as having no more sorrow or pain as we are told in the Book of Revelation, "He'll wipe every tear from their eyes, and death shall be no more — no more grief, or crying out or pain, for what came before has passed away" (21:4). All this is true, but the really important thing is that we shall be changed inwardly. All selfish, fearful, cowardly, impatient inclinations will be destroyed in us and we will be reprogrammed with inclinations and instincts that have nothing in them but love.God is all love and we will be transformed in God. Born anew!

In resurrection the prayer of Jesus when he pleaded with his Father will be finally answered: that beautiful prayer at the Last Supper "that all may be one, as you, Father, are in me, and I in you" (Jn 17:21). This is the divine, or divinized life of which Paul is speaking in this connection. The dark side of mystical death is the letting go of the self-satisfactions that keep us from loving. The bright side is the transformation into love that is even here on earth the beginning of heaven.

CHAPTER 18

Relating to Others

P aul was a practical man. Even though he was a mystic and wrote much about relating one-on-one with God in personal prayer he also had much to say about down-to-earth relating to others. For him, prayer and relating to others were connected. Anyone who was really listening to the Lord in prayer was bound to act lovingly towards others. There would be human failings, of course, but prayer would help with those too, and would bring about progress in Christ-like love and in extending this love to others.

Paul's primary approach to prayer, as we have seen, was to meditate on the Passion and to see and hear there the tremendous love of God. The next step was to translate mutual love for God into mutual love for others. He writes to Mother Mary Crucified when she was superior of the Passionist Nuns, "Encourage in the community the shining forth of holy love that they may love one another mutually, that they may have compassion on one another, that they may help one another in their needs. To sum up: that the true spirit of the Crucified should shine forth" (II, 323).

Love is Primary

Love was always primary in Paul's mind. He writes to his own brothers and sisters, "Always keep in mind that most holy commandment of love which Jesus gave to his disciples before going to his death, there at the Last Supper. He said to them, 'My dear apostles, I give you a new commandment, that you should love one another as I have loved you' (Jn 15:12)! Oh, WHAT BEAUTIFUL WORDS! The example is clear. Love one another, love one another, my most dear brothers and sisters. Remember that you will never please God if you do not love one another. Let there be no dissension among you. If occasionally a sharp word slips, immediately soften it. Let no reproach take hold of your heart or govern your speech" (I, 56-57).

Paul reminded his own religious community of the same thing 53 years later when approaching his death: "First of all I recommend most earnestly the observance of that most holy reminder given by Jesus to his disciples, 'By this will all know that you are my disciples if you love one another" (Jn 13:25) (Processes III, 491).

All Paul's recommendations to those he directed had love as the primary goal: relating to God in deep mutual love and expressing this love by pouring it out on others. If Paul spoke of prayer, it was as a love-conversation with God; if he spoke of penance, it was as a purification of the heart for deeper love; if he spoke of death, it was a death to self to become more capable of love. We can understand the many negative warnings in Paul's direction only if we see the positive goal of it all, which was total love.

Paul wrote to Agnes, "Draw love of God from every creature, but to do this well, it is necessary to be detached from them, even dead to them.... Love everyone in God but don't be attached to anyone" (I, 110). It is possible to interpret statements like this by Paul and others of his era as a recommendation to have only a generic love for others and never one that is deeply personal. Doubtless many have acted this way in their relationships to others. But does Paul mean this? He certainly did not act that way himself.

Loving "in God"

Paul says to love everyone "in God" and to be detached. As we have seen before, detachment is really detachment from self and from our own self-satisfaction, chiefly in people. We are all naturally attracted to some, and are repelled in various degrees by others. Paul is really saying, as so many other mystics, saints and spiritual writers have said, that our natural attractions and aversions have nothing to do with love which is "in God."

To love someone "in God" is not to love with a coldly impersonal love, but to love as God does. God's love is not the response to an attraction, as our natural human love is. God's love originates with himself. He loves because he chooses to love. He loves freely and pours it out on the way he chooses to each one. To love "in God" is loving in this same way. God empowers us by his Holy Spirit to be able to love as he does if we allow the Spirit to move us. Our hearts can learn to love freely by choosing to love others, even where there is no natural attraction to begin with, or when there is no response to the love we pour out.

Jesus speaks of this kind of love when he says, "Love your enemies, pray for your persecutors. This will prove that you are sons of your heavenly Father, for his sun rises on the bad and the good, he rains on the just and the unjust. If you love those who love you, what merit is there in that? Do not tax collectors do as much? And if you greet your brothers only, what is so praiseworthy about that? Do not pagans do as much? In a word, you must be perfect as your heavenly Father is perfect" (Mt 5:44-48).

How God Loves

Here Jesus is speaking of the contrast between the natural human love of which we are all capable, and the way the Father loves. Our love is a response to an attraction, and when that attraction is not there, we are not inclined to love. God's love begins in his own freedom, his own choice. He chooses to love and keeps doing it independently of any response or lack of it. Naturally, he can pour out more where there is more receptivity, and we can too. But God continues to love even when there is no response. As Jesus says, he pours it out on the just and the unjust.

When we look at the love Jesus showed others, we notice that he showed it very differently in different situations. Sometimes he was warm and tender, sometimes strong and challenging. He responded quickly to some requests and refused others.

He tried to please others as far as he could, but he was no doormat. He did not go along with what everyone wanted of him in the name of love. When love demanded that he say a strong "No" to some, he did so. When love told Him to yield, He did that too, as the case of the Canaanite woman shows us (Mk 7:24-30).

We cannot love as Jesus does by our own unaided power. That is why we have been given the Holy Spirit. As Paul the apostle puts it, 'The love of God has been poured into our hearts by the Holy Spirit, who has been given to us" (Rm 5:5). Only by the power of the Spirit can we love where there is no natural attraction or no response. We too can love more and give more love where there is more receptivity and more response, but we cannot pour out love where there is little or no receptivity and little or no response except in the power of the Spirit. This is loving with the perfect love the Father has. We will certainly not love in this perfect way in our lifetime, but we must always be moving in this direction. We must take the Father's love as our model and goal. This is what Paul of the Cross means by loving "in God." This is why he tells us we need to be detached from our own natural attractions and repugnances.

Multiple Relationships

Another recommendation of Paul to Agnes in this regard which has often been misinterpreted is this: "Show yourself the same to all, but don't enter into particular friendships" (I, 110). If we just look at the expression, "particular friendship," it seems that every friendship has to be particular and unique. But that expression came to have a technical meaning. It meant a friendship with one person that shut others out, an exclusive friendship which did not encourage relationships with others and was filled with jealousy and possessiveness. Friendships and relationships "in God" are not jealous and possessive friendships but are open to all, though in a uniquely different way to each.

It may help to repeat here what Paul wrote to Agnes about his own varied relationships to others, which we quoted back in the first chapter. He says, "I love all souls, and especially those whom God has entrusted to me for spiritual direction. My soul experiences a completely spiritual bond which binds it more strongly to one soul, less so to another, according to the greater or lesser love to which God has called that soul. Let me explain what I mean. If one soul has reached a higher degree of love and union with God than another, then (as God has given me to understand it) I am certain that, just as that soul is more loved by the Supreme Good, so the bond of charity links my soul more closely with it. But that does not mean that it is not united in charity with others also, but more with one, less with another, as the Supreme Good wishes it" (I, 149).

Perhaps today we might be less inclined to use the mathematical comparison that Paul uses, e.g. more and less, which imply quantity. We might be more inclined to use a qualitative comparison. We might say that God wants us to love each one uniquely and differently.

Non-Exclusive Relationships

This unique love can become very deep and intimate. After all, it is a love that is empowered by the Spirit to be a reflection of God's love. This kind of love is not at all understood by our time and culture. It is presumed unquestioningly that for love to be deep and intimate, it has to be exclusive. The one loved has to be the only one. If there is another involved, it becomes a triangle that ends up in turmoil. If there are even more involved, the problems can become astronomical. Yet Jesus never formed his followers into pairs of lovers, of which marriage is the model, but into a community of love with everyone loving everyone else in the most intimate love. Certainly even for Jesus, this must have been a long-range goal, but he makes it clear that we must be willing to head in this direction.

One reason for the problem in all this is that it is presumed in our culture that all love is jealous and possessive, and in fact probably most loves are that way. To have an intimate love-relationship with more than one person that is open, non-possessive, non-exclusive, and true to each love, is unthinkable in our society. Yet this is the type of relationship that Paul of the Cross is speaking of with those God gave him to love and the type of relationship Jesus prayed that we all might one day come to when he prayed to his Father, "That all maybe one, Father, as you are in me and I in you" (Jn 17:21). Such relationships demand great willingness to die to self and to be open to give of oneself. We know from the saints that such relationships are possible.

"Soul" and "Person"

In speaking of relationships, Paul often uses the word "soul," his soul relating to the soul of the one he directed. Paul's use of the word "soul" is different from what we might say today, though many still use this expression. Spiritual writers of Paul's time and for many centuries before used the word "soul" to mean "person." However, when that terminology was used, it was hard to avoid giving the impression that the body did not enter the situation and was not part of the "spiritual life." The word "soul" as a counterpart to "body" was taken from medieval scholastic philosophy and was based on Aristotle's distinction (four centuries before Christ) between "soul" and "body" as two components of a human person. But Sacred Scripture, which was not based on Aristotle's philosophy and which spoke in Hebrew thought patterns, does not make any such distinction and speaks of the whole person when it uses the word "soul." To be more faithful to scriptural usage, we might say, not that God wants us to love all "souls" but all "persons." However, it is good to remember that when Paul speaks of this love "in God" he is not speaking of a cold, generic love, but of "bonding" with others. This is an expression about which much is being written today. Love "in God" is real love, not an ethereal dehumanized kind of love.

"Charity" and "Love"

Another word that Paul and others of his time use when speaking of love which might be a little confusing today is the word "charity." This word comes from the Greek and means "love." Since the New Testament was originally written in Greek, this word is often used to describe the love we should have for others in God. The famous chapter 13 of First Corinthians uses this word extensively. However, today the word "charity" is often used primarily of almsgiving. If we would understand what Paul and other spiritual writers mean by "charity," we have to understand it as a love such as God has for us.

Overcoming Aversions

Such a love includes, as Jesus says, loving our enemies. St. Thérèse makes this particular application, "There are, of course, no enemies here in the convent. But there can be an attraction towards one and a temptation to go a long way around to avoid meeting another...Jesus teaches me that this is the one I need to love" (Ste. Thérèse de Lisieux, Manuscrits autobiographiques, Carmel de Lisieux, p. 271). It is easy to love those we like and to think we are doing it for God. The test as St. Thérèse makes clear is to concentrate on those to whom we are not naturally attracted and we will have no trouble with the others.

Paul of the Cross makes a similar application in writing to Agnes, "The aversions which you experience, the ridicule, the scorn, the jokes at your expense, and so forth, should be received with great gratitude toward God. They serve as the pyre of love on which the victim of love is consumed. Gently drive away all aversions and show yourself cordial to everyone. I leave you free to do as God will show you" (I, 107). Many who are striving for a closer union with God and want to love everyone get very discouraged when they find aversions for certain others. They think it is a bad sign, and that they can never learn to love such persons. Yet that is precisely why the power of the Holy Spirit has been given to us: to enable us to love where it is humanly impossible. He can teach us to love even those our human hearts would naturally reject. The message of Jesus is clear on this point and Paul of the Cross, along with many other saints, emphasized it strongly.

Paul gives this recommendation to Sister Cheruhina Bresciani, who was having trouble with a Sister who did not like her: "That Sister was wrong in not wanting to come into your room. However, learn to have compassion on her. Speak to her with love, but a love accompanied by a reserve and a seriousness that fits the particular situation. Look at her in the side of Jesus Christ, and in this way, you will love her with a pure and holy love. If she comes into the room, don't be annoyed, but accept it, and say a few words to her. Then recollect yourself in God in holy silence. When you are praying in chapel, look at her more than ever in the heart of Jesus Christ, and let go of any feeling of anger. Say to your heart, 'My heart, love this dear Sister! Love her who is the image of your God! Love her, my heart, in the blood of Jesus Christ! O my poor Sister, I love you in God! I have compassion on you! I no longer want to be annoyed with you!' Say all this in spirit and gently. If you fall into some resentment, follow it up by asking pardon. Above all, don't be upset over it, but humble yourself gently before God. If you fall this way, you are not disobedient to me and there is no sin" (I, 437).

In this recommendation to Sister Cherubina, Paul shows her how to make her prayer life both a remedy for her resentment of that other Sister and a source of love. Notice, too, how he gently tries to keep her from putting herself on a guilt trip if she found that she could not immediately overcome all aversion for this Sister. Paul knew well that victories over resentments like these demand a long struggle and we need much patience with ourselves.

Notice that Paul encourages Sister Cherubina to speak to that other Sister with "a love accompanied by reserve." Love does not always mean being warmly affectionate toward the other person. It has to mean reserve at times and even sometimes confrontation, especially if the other person is trying to take advantage of us. Love does not mean being a doormat. Jesus was no doormat and neither was Paul. To let others "use" us in the manipulative sense is not love and no good for them or for us. The Holy Spirit has to teach us when to be warm and outwardly friendly and when to be reserved and firm.

Seeing God in Others

Even though Paul's primary resource in everything was prayer, he also suggests a course of action at times that would meet the approval of modern psychology. Paul writes to Agnes concerning a person with whom she had difficulty: "The truth is that she is a good person, and if she says something that is hard to take, it comes from the oppression of a poor spirit afflicted and battered. Therefore we must take it all in good part" (I, 309). Here Paul looks not only at the actions of the other person, but tries to discover or at least surmise the causes of these actions. He can tell that she had been wounded in the past. He may not use modern techniques of enneagrams, dream analysis, or Meyers -Briggs tests to try to discover these causes, but he is aware that the causes are there and he believes that compassion is the best way to help what he calls "a spirit battered and afflicted." The countless battered women and abused children of today would find a friend in him.

On one occasion, Paul felt that he had to reproach Mother Mary Crucified for not having a loving and forgiving attitude towards those who had accused her falsely. He quotes her as writing to him, "What a suffering! What torment! I have to serve my accusers!" Then he answers, "This shows that you have little, very little virtue, because one of the greatest graces the Lord has given you is to provide the present occasion of exercising true humility of heart, true patience and gentleness, and above all, a great love towards these persons, looking at them as most noble instruments used by God to enrich your soul with virtues" (II, 296).

The more indirect psychological approaches of today (that of Carl Rogers, for example) might not square with such a blunt approach as Paul used, but this approach was at least effective. We cannot judge a man who lived in the eighteenth century by awarenesses that have come to light only in the twentieth, but the results show that Paul's approach bore fruit. Mother Mary Crucified continued to use Paul as her spiritual director and grew greatly in her interior life through him.

Paul may not have been as aware of the feelings of those to whom he was writing as we are apt to be today, especially of the feelings of women, but his faith insights are as valid today as they were then. He saw everything from the viewpoint of God's loving providential care, as we have already seen. From that viewpoint, those who were making trouble for Mother Mary Crucified were God's instruments for her purification and growth. But she was doing what all of us tend to do.

She was looking at what others were doing and saying and presuming God had nothing to do with the situation.

For Paul, there could be no situation with which God had nothing to do. God has a hand in everything and his love for us never lets anything get out of his control. We need to learn to accept the cup from the hands of the Father as Jesus did, and not from the hands of others. Accepting it from the hands of others, or taking it as if it came only from their hands, makes it more bitter. Accepting it from the loving hand of the Father makes it easier and sweeter all the time.

Paul would see a situation like this as another example of what Jesus meant when He told us to love our enemies. Obviously, this is impossible to our unaided human nature, but not to the love-power the Holy Spirit gives us when we are willing.

Our Need to Share

Even though Paul emphasized detachment from others, this meant, as we have seen, detachment from self-seeking in others. He did speak of avoiding others when mutual association would not benefit either party at the moment. But Paul did not mean keeping away from others when the Holy Spirit indicated that there should be sharing. Paul wrote to Lucy Burlini, "I hope that by the mercy of God, I will have an opportunity for a visit with you in which God may give us the lights to share on the unspeakable beauty of his love. I have not forgotten other visits we had with opportunities to share together in Jesus Christ" (II, 717).

In a similar vein Paul wrote to Thomas Fossi about sharing with his wife, "I thank God that she is so patient in suffering, as you tell me. It is good to discuss with one another your interior sufferings and other spiritual matters. This will be useful and give pleasure to God. But don't just give in to the complaints of nature. Nature does not understand what God is doing" (I, 580). The purpose of detachment from others is not to keep us away from them, but to free us from self-seeking so that we can share more closely and intimately with others.

Marital Relations

Paul was a practical man, as we have seen. He often treats of matters we would not expect to hear about from a mystic. One example is sexual expression in marriage. At Paul's time, virginity, or consecrated celibacy, was considered the ideal way to follow Christ and marriage only a secondary, less holy road. Thomas Fossi presumed this notion without question, as did others of his time. He was constantly pleading with Paul, who was his spiritual director, to OK his desire to practice sexual continence in marriage. We might expect an ascetic like Paul to applaud the idea, but it was just the opposite. Even though Thomas kept up his entreaties for about 30 years, Paul would never agree that this was a good idea. Let us look at a couple of Paul's observations in the matter.

"A resolution to maintain conjugal continence is hardly a good idea. Both spouses should be free and leave each other free. In this way, love is better preserved, and the way is closed to many temptations from the devil, especially to jealousy. If your wife says she wants what you do, it may be more from modesty than from real desire. Stay free in this area" (I, 554). Paul had no Jansenistic or Puritanical views of marriage. He saw marriage as good, and this included sexual expression. His positive view of this, so rare at the time, not too common even in our own time, he expressed in another letter to Thomas. "Sexual expression in marriage with the holy intention that should go with it does not prevent a couple from becoming saints right in their own state. Look at the many holy men and women who are married. Keep your heart recollected and remain interiorly in the divine presence" (I, 564). For Paul, the body was good and holy. The important thing was to keep recollected, that is, to keep listening to the Lord, and to let all bodily actions be directed by the Holy Spirit.

As we can see now, Paul saw all relationships to others and all actions flowing from such relationships as coming from prayer, that is, from a life of constant, intimate communion with God. His principles were simply an application of what Sacred Scripture has already said in this regard, "He who loves God, should love his brother too" (Jn 4:21).

CHAPTER 19

The Fruits of a Life of Prayer

There are many difficulties in a life of prayer, which is the Christian life lived in depth and in constant communication with God. While Paul of the Cross never down-played these trials, he never wanted those he directed to focus on them. He preferred instead to focus on the fruits of a life of prayer. As Jesus expressed it to his disciples at the Last Supper, "I have designated you to go and bear fruit, and that your fruit should endure" (Jn 15:16). Paul believed we could find much encouragement from looking at these fruits. They are the glorious qualities, virtues and effects in each person which make him or her most pleasing in the eyes of God. Let us consider these fruits to find our own encouragement by looking at the goal of our journey and not merely focusing on the hardships we meet with on the way.

Love, the First Fruit

The primary fruit for Paul of the Cross was God's love. He writes to Teresa Palozzi, "May God grant you the great gift of holy love, which is the treasure of treasures" (III, 356). True love, according to St. Thomas Aquinas is something mutual. With God's love, though, the important thing is not our love for him, but his love for us. As we read in the Scriptures, "This is what love is: not that we loved God, but that he loved us and sent his Son as the expiation for our sins" (1 Jn 4:10). Paul speaks often of this dimension of love. He writes to Mrs. Nicolina Martinez, "In prayer, remain before God, entirely plunged into his love" (I, 41). In modern parlance, we might say, "Let yourself fall in love with God." We can do this only when we plunge into his love for us and allow his love to penetrate and fill us. Paul frequently uses the expression "getting drunk" on God's love. He writes to Agnes Grazi, "Drink of that wine which the Supreme Good will give you and never stop drinking. If you get drunk, it doesn't matter. This holy drunkenness will make you wise, humble and entirely of God" (I, 291).

It might seem wonderful to let ourselves be loved by God, but it is very difficult. Many good Christians do their best to love God, but it is hard for them to believe that he loves them and is pleased with them, even in spite of their faults. Paul writes to Mother Mary Crucified, "You have signs clearer than the day that God loves you and that this work is entirely his" (II, 293). The signs may be clearer than the noonday sun for us too, but it is still hard to believe that God is so deeply in love with us, especially if we have just fallen into some fault or become conscious of some failing we had never noticed before. We have to come to believe that God loves us unconditionally and that he will always love us, no matter what.

When Paul of the Cross uses the comparison of drinking from the breast of God, which we considered in detail in Chapter 10, he is speaking of drinking in God's love and allowing ourselves to be loved by God. A baby at its mother's breast doesn't worry about being unworthy or about trying hard to earn or deserve the milk. It simply trusts that the milk will always be there when it is needed. This is one of the points of comparison Paul makes in this example.

He often mixes metaphors in this comparison and sometimes speaks of drinking milk from the breast of God, and at other times of drinking wine there. For him, both are metaphors for God's love. What he is really saying is that if you engage in a life of prayer, you will find it easier and easier to let God love you and to relax in his love and enjoy it.

Wisdom

In the words of Paul to Agnes quoted above, we notice a few of the virtues which Paul believed came from a life of prayer. He speaks of wisdom. This is not a wisdom that comes from study or deep intellectual reflection. It is a gift of God. It is the wisdom Paul the apostle speaks of when he says, "The Spirit we have received is not the spirit of this world but the Spirit which comes from God and enables us to know what it is that God has freely bestowed on us. And we proclaim this in words taught by the Spirit rather than by human wisdom, words which explain spiritual matters to those who have the Spirit" (1 Cor 2:12-13) . He identifies this wisdom with "Christ crucified, a stumbling block for Jews and foolishness for Greeks, but to those who have been chosen, Jews and Greeks alike, Christ, the power of God and the wisdom of God" (1 Cor 1:23-24) . This was exactly what Paul of the Cross was referring to in his letter to Agnes, when he tells her that she will drink wisdom. He is speaking of drinking from the side of Christ on the cross.

This wisdom gives a new way of looking at things, a new and deeper faith-perspective. It sees God's hand in everything and looks at events, not just with their natural causes, as might be done, for example, on a TV news broadcast, but looks at these events in the light of faith to try to understand how God's love is directing them. To leave this love out in looking at any event is not to see the whole of reality. The wisdom of the cross enables us to penetrate the meaning of events far more deeply than the eye can observe.

Humility

Paul also speaks of humility in that passage to Agnes. Humility enables us to look at ourselves in truth as we are before God. It recognizes our faults, but sees them in God's mercy and is at peace over them. It recognizes our virtues and other qualities and abilities, but sees them as God's gifts and therefore does not try to flaunt them before others as if they were our own. Paul the apostle asks this question, "What do you have that you didn't receive? And if you have received it, why are you boasting as if it were yours alone?" (1 Cor 4:7). Humility keeps us from becoming depressed by our faults and inflated by our qualities.

Paul of the Cross speaks of this humility in stronger terms in another letter to Agnes. He says, "Let me explain a little the graces which are produced by prayer and which remain in the soul afterwards. They leave and produce a deep self-forgetfulness which brings about a desire to be despised and scorned by all, forgotten by all. Also a perfect union with the divine will" (I, 253). Paul was not speaking in modern psychological terms when he spoke of "self-forgetfulness" or "self-annihilation." He was speaking of the destruction of that tendency to pride and self-seeking which is so strong within us. He is using language similar to other mystics such as John of the Cross and Teresa of Avila, who speak of becoming nothing that God may be our all. This is not something we can bring about ourselves, but is the fruit of a life of prayer and surrender to God.

Peace

In this same letter to Agnes, Paul speaks of "death to all that is not God," an expression that John Tauler frequently uses. Paul speaks of the fruit of that death as "a continual remembrance of the supreme good, which produces in the soul a great calm and peace in God" (I, 253). This is the peace Jesus spoke of to his disciples at the Last Supper, "Peace I leave with you; my peace I give to you. Not as the world gives do I give to you. Do not let your hearts be troubled or afraid" (Jn 14:27). The world can give peace, only when it can make outward circumstances calm, such as by a treaty of peace after a war, successful surgery after an appendicitis attack, or the transfer of an annoying fellow worker to another plant. The world, meaning human efforts unaided by God, cannot always make outward circumstances peaceful, nor can it give that deep inner peace Jesus was speaking of. Notice that he spoke of giving his peace when about to enter his Passion, the most unpeaceful outward situation we can imagine. The peace Jesus gives lasts not only while the waters are calm, but even when they become troubled. Only Jesus can give this kind of peace. Paul of the Cross calls it one of the fruits of prayer. He speaks of it as something infused, that is, poured into the soul by God (I, 2).

Self-Control

In a letter to Sister Columba Gandolfi Paul speaks of other fruits of prayer for which she should look. One of them which most of us would find very helpful is control of the passions (II, 455). When theologians speak of the passions, they mean the emotions, the feelings, especially of the power we tend to give our feelings to control us. Paul speaks especially of anger, fears and desires. The fruit of prayer in this regard is to give us freedom from the domination of our feelings, so that we can act as the Holy Spirit is indicating to us and not be blown around by the wind of every feeling that arises.

Patience

In this same letter, Paul speaks of patience. Patience includes the ability to wait for God's timing when we want things to happen right away. Waiting is one of the hardest things for us mortals to do, especially if we are suffering or even just uncomfortable, ill at ease, bored, or expectant in any way. No matter how hard we try, we cannot make ourselves be patient under all circumstances. This patience is a gift of God and one of the fruits of prayer.

Missionary Zeal

One of the most important fruits of prayer on which Paul places special emphasis is "having ardent desires for the glory of God and the salvation of souls" (I, 329). Another way he puts it is this, "a most ardent love of God and of the neighbor" (I, 253). These fruits are put together by Paul, since he saw them as two facets of the same reality. The more God's love was imbibed in prayer the more the desire to respond to that love would grow. He saw that desire as a longing to have God loved and accepted by everybody. He felt it himself most strongly and believed that everyone who led a life of prayer in depth would experience it too.

From this passionate love for God flowed the desire to lead others to him, "souls" as the common expression was in those days. Paul's prayer was never a selfish "navel-gazing," but included an awareness of all whom God loved. Paul longed to bring others to respond to that love. He believed that all true prayer, whatever form it took, would have this effect. He himself founded a religious congregation, the Passionists, which would reach out to other people, bringing them the message of God's love through the Passion and attracting them to surrender to that love. He also gave the same message to contemplative nuns who never left their convents. He believed that all true prayer led to a deep concern for others and their eternal welfare, no matter what condition or state of life the one who prayed had embraced. This same attitude was strongly expressed a century later by a contemplative nun, St. Thérèse of Lisieux, whose desire to reach out to bring others to God was so strong, even though she never left her cloister, that she has been declared by the Church a patroness of the missions alongside of St. Francis Xavier, who brought thousands to the Christian faith in the Far East. For Paul this particular fruit of prayer was not limited to spreading the faith to unbelievers or converting sinners, but sincerely loving all those God puts into our lives. We have spoken of this in the chapter on relationships to others.

By no means does Paul ever intend to give a complete list of the fruits of prayer. It would take volumes for that. He only gives a few samples to encourage those he is directing.

Fruits of Satan

In speaking of the fruits of prayer, Paul occasionally contrasts them with other fruits which he calls the fruits of Satan. He gives some samples in a letter to Sister Cherubina Bresciani. After speaking of the fruits of prayer given by God, such as knowledge of God, awareness of one's own nothingness, detachment from all that is not God, love for the cross, peace, desire for prayer, and so forth, Paul speaks of the works of Satan. "The works of the devil, on the contrary, seem at first to bring some peace and devotion, but it does not last, and it generates a secret presumption and an inflated idea of oneself, disturbance of spirit and the arousing of feelings that are hard to control, close-mindedness, attachment to one's own opinions, a lessening of esteem for others and a concern for one's own appearance; these and other effects are occasioned by the work of the devil" (I, 443). Paul did not want the Sister to be afraid but to be aware of what could happen when anyone engaged in prayer for one's own glorification.

Paul also speaks of some of the signs that many take as indications of going backwards or not praying well and shows that they are no signs at all. He writes to Teresa Palozzi, "Even though in prayer, you experience absence of any feeling of devotion and also coldness, have patience. Bear this with resignation and stay at prayer for the full time you had decided to pray, even though it seems that your prayer is not fruitful. This is not the case" (III, 381). It is the usual thing for those who walk the way of the Lord to experience much dryness and emptiness, especially when there had been great feelings of devotion previously. Paul wanted those he directed to know that these are not bad signs and are to be expected.

Heaven

The final fruit of a life of prayer is heaven itself. Paul had some beautiful things to say about it. He wrote to Agnes when she was sick and it looked as if she might not recover. "Leave yourself in freedom to aspire to that glory which through the infinite merits of Jesus has been prepared for you. Oh, how necessary it is to open the way that you may desire and desire more that beautiful paradise where we will be always in an eternal feast, praising our supreme good unceasingly without any more danger of ever losing him!" (I, 239). In speaking of heaven, Paul focuses on God, whom he loved so dearly. But he implicitly includes the presence of others in speaking of a feast. A feast is something in which many partake and enjoy each other as well as their host. Sacred Scripture several times uses the image of a feast to speak of the future life.

Paul loved Agnes and included her in his idea of heaven. On one occasion he really gets carried away and rhapsodizes on his expectations of heaven. "Oh, what holy thoughts I have had today while I was walking! Thoughts of love and union with God for my soul and for your soul.

O true God, what will become of our hearts when we swim in the infinite sea of your sweetness!

What will happen, when up there in heaven we will be entirely transformed through love into God, when we will be satisfied with that infinite Good of which God himself is our contentment!

What will it be like, my daughter, when we will sing in eternity the divine mercies, the triumphs of the Immaculate Lamb and of Mary our most holy mother!

What will it be like when we shall sing without ceasing the eternal Holy, Holy, Holy, when together with the saints we will sing that most sweet Alleluia! What will our hearts be like, our spirits! When we will be united to God more than iron is united to fire, which without ceasing to be iron, yet seems to be all fire. In this way we will be totally transformed in God, so that our soul will be totally divinized. Oh, when will we see that day! When, when will death burst the walls of our prison! Ah, that will be the day of our espousals, of our nuptials, in which our soul in a most sublime way will be espoused to our dear Jesus and will sit in eternity at the heavenly banquet" (I, 194-195).

Paul longed for heaven, not as an escape, but to be finally united with his God in love and to be with all others who were also so united. This desire was a real experience for him, as we might gather from his ecstatic words to Agnes. He wanted not only Agnes, but all those he directed to experience the same longing for heaven and union with God, and not the fear of death that most people experience. He looked at death as the entrance to his wedding celebration. A wedding celebration is a most attractive image, often used in Scripture, and implying love and joy and not fear. In reality, human marriage does not usually turn out so blissfully, but it is still a good sign and image of our final union with God. For Paul, this was not merely a literary image, but a reality in his life. He wanted all those he directed to have the same experience. He believed it would come as they were faithful to their lives of prayer.

May Paul's guidance be a help to us too as we journey towards our final goal. May our life of prayer become more and more a courtship, as we allow Jesus to win our hearts. May his Holy Spirit bring us all to our own personal fullness of life and love.